Slave to a Job, Master of Your Career

Slave to a Job,
Master of your Career

Sean McLoughney

Chartered
Accountants
Ireland

Published by
Chartered Accountants Ireland
Chartered Accountants House
47–49 Pearse Street
Dublin 2
www.charteredaccountants.ie

This publication is designed to provide accurate and authoritative information in regard to the subject matter covered. It is provided on the understanding that Chartered Accountants Ireland is not engaged in rendering professional services. If professional advice or other expert assistance is required, the services of a competent professional should be sought.

ISBN 978-0-903854-96-2

Typeset by Marsha Swan
Printed by ColourBooks, Ireland

To Carol for all your support,
and Alex and Rachel for being the best two girls in the world.

CONTENTS

PREFACE AND ACKNOWLEDGEMENTS

I would love to say that my career started as a result of careful planning but, like so many people, it began with a mixture of luck and just old fashioned 'knowing someone'.

In the bleak employment days of 1981, when I was a 6th year student in St Declan's College in Dublin, my career in EBS Building Society began in a fortuitous way. On a wet Wednesday afternoon I was reluctantly on my way to a geography class, when I bumped into my good friend Colm O'Connor who, though also due to attend the same class, was heading in the opposite direction.

– "Where are you going?" I inquired

– "I'm off to do an interview with the EBS", he replied, laughing

– "You're doing what?"

– "A job interview."

As I pondered whether I should go to my class or have a laugh doing a mock interview (at the time I didn't even realise it was a real interview with a real job on offer) my career suddenly began there and then. I decided that the interview was a better option, so I followed Colm to the room where the interviews would take place. My next problem was to get my name onto to the list as they had shortlisted a number of candidates. Then luck intervened, because David Earle was conducting the interviews and he happened to be a friend of mine. Not only did I get an interview but, after a few more interviews at EBS Head Office, I managed to get a job. David continued to play an important role in my career within EBS.

Throughout my career, I have been very lucky to be mentored by some great people and great managers. David Earle, Tommy Kiernan, Kevin O'Reilly, Michael Mooney and Gerry Middleton showed me what it took to perform at the highest levels and why you should plan your career. I still remember their words of wisdom and the times that Dave Harris and Diarmuid Boyle would take me aside and point out quietly the things that I needed to change. Perhaps the best piece of advice came from Dave Keenan who explained in a simple but brilliant way the need to continually develop yourself because "the day when no one else wants you is the day we (EBS) won't want you either". He delivered this message just days after I got my first big promotion.

Although the EBS was my first job, my career started when I was 13 years' old working in my aunt's shop in Templederry, County Tipperary. Here I learnt what customer service and care is all about. Both Tom and Bernie showed me the meaning of valuing customers and how to build loyalty. I also remember Donal Ryan (Donal Ryan Motor Group) explaining how to win a customer for life and why you should be passionate about your customers. These lessons are still with me today and are included in this book.

If the first part of career was largely due to luck, the second part of my career was planned. After almost 20 years working with some great people in EBS, it was time to start doing something that I love and enjoy. That's when I decided to set up Learning Curve and to have fun working with people to help them improve how they manage them-selves and those around them. It was during the early years of Learning Curve that the idea for this book, *Slave to a Job, Master of your Career*, started to take shape. After working with a number of different organisations to help them improve the performance of their staff, it became clear that the key to high performance was to encourage staff to change their way of thinking from that of an employee to that of an entrepreneur. This shift in mindset proved to be pivotal in improving performance levels. Some early success with a course designed with the help of Dave Kilmartin encouraged me to develop this idea further and over the last number of years I have used the principles outlined here in various successful training courses.

All careers need support and the best support comes from your family. My parents, Sean and Anne, have supported my career from day one and they both set a great example of how to work ethically and professionally, to always treat your customers with respect and to exceed their expectations. They are the best role models that anyone could wish to have. Also my wife Carol has always shown great faith throughout the ups and downs of a self-employed professional. Without her support, Learning Curve would not be the success it is today.

My career in writing started with Kieran Lyons, whose great energy and passion was the support I needed to write my first book, *Slave to the Clock, Master of Time*. His unwavering support got me over the finishing line.

Every book has a team of people working behind the scenes to make it happen. I am eternally grateful to Michael Diviney (Director of Publishing) for first agreeing with my idea for this book and for his tireless work, challenging me to make it better. Michael's determination and attention to detail drove this project on and kept me focused on the end result. I would also like to thank Lucy Taylor for her editing work, Elizabeth MacAulay for her proof-reading and Marsha Swan, who once again did a brilliant job on bringing the book alive with her design. As always, I'm indebted to Agnieszka Pobedynska, who kept the project moving along and ensured that I met my deadlines.

I would also like to thank the countless people who took part in the research for the book, who answered my many e-mails and who have attended my training courses over the years. Their continuous endorsement of my training methods and ideas keep me inspired and loving this job of mine. My thanks also to all the companies that I have worked with and for their continued support. I hope you enjoy the book and, most of all, I hope you remain employable and are a **Master of your Career**.

CHAPTER I
IT'S YOUR CAREER:
MANAGING YOURSELF LIKE A BUSINESS

Quick guide to this chapter

- You are not just an employee
- You own your career
- Consider yourself to be an attractive business
- Who are your customers?
- Have a makeover
- Manage your career using the same skills that you employ to manage your work
- Build a framework to manage your career
- Every business has its departments
- Your Personal Vision
- Your Personal Vision Statement

The news comes as a shock. It's like hearing of the death of a sick relative. Although you had known that they were seriously ill for some time, you were still not prepared for the news that they are gone. There's numbness, and a sense of resigned acceptance: a short statement confirms the rumours that your employer is closing down immediately and you are now out of work!

This is a new experience for you, one that you never thought would happen. Initially, you feel shock and anger.

"It is not the strongest of the species that survives, nor the most intelligent, but the one most responsive to change."

Charles Darwin

I

You say goodbye to work colleagues and friends, and as you leave you look at your old world for the last time. You now face a new uncertain future, for which you are totally unprepared. It will be stressful and challenging, but when you get to grips with your new circumstances it will become exciting.

For some people losing their job is akin to losing their identity, their self worth. It is a dramatic experience. As unemployment levels rise, more and more people are faced with the daunting prospect of finding work in a shrinking jobs market. For many, job hunting in today's environment is a new experience. They don't have the skills required to give them an advantage in the race to unearth the few jobs that are available. Nor do they have the vision and foresight to prepare themselves for future work prospects. They allow frustration and negativity to replace determination and a proactive approach to finding work, which, in turn, leads to many missed opportunities. They waste too much time and energy in self pity and thinking about the past. They are entrenched in their self-limiting employee mindset.

This negative mindset is not confined to people who have lost their jobs. It is also rampant among those who are *still employed*! Unfortunately, far too many people are prompted to think about their careers for negative reasons. These might include:

- I'm stressed out because of my workload
- I can't stand my boss
- I don't get on with my colleagues
- There are no jobs out there
- The wages are poor here
- I'm earning less but expected to do more
- I didn't work hard at getting my qualification to end up doing this type of work
- My career is going nowhere
- There are no promotional prospects here
- My job is boring
- Things don't look well for my company
- Some of my colleagues have been let go
- I didn't get my bonus this year

As unemployment levels rise, more and more people are faced with the daunting prospect of finding work in a shrinking jobs market. For many, job hunting in today's environment is a new experience.

This negative mindset is not confined to people who have lost their jobs. It is also rampant among those who are *still employed*! Unfortunately, far too many people are prompted to think about their careers for negative reasons.

The list is endless, but it illustrates that most people only review their careers when they are in crisis management mode. This runs the risk that you will make life-changing decisions when you are in a negative mindset. Imagine running a business based on the same criteria: no plan or direction, just drifting along stuck in your own little world —only thinking about the company's future when something drastic goes wrong. Do you think you would stay in business for very long managing on such a crisis basis?

To become a master of today's overcrowded job market you need to **change from crisis management to strategic management**. You need to change your mindset, become a visionary and look at the factors that make *you* different, competitive and capable of winning work. Transfer the principles of strategic management into the business of running your career and you can start to appreciate the similarities.

Most people only review their careers when they are in crisis management mode.

A change in your mindset

A new business world has arrived and with it comes change and new workplace models that require a shift in people's mindsets. The days of being just an employee, doing the same job for 20 years or more, are gone, and are unlikely to return. New ways of thinking, problem-solving and understanding both customer's and employer's needs are now being demanded. Fashions come and go, trends come and go, and jobs come and go. What were once deemed vibrant and "must have" jobs are now seen as cast-offs in this changing business environment. And this has happened in a flash. Change is part of our working life.

Throughout Europe and America, unemployment in traditional business sectors is on the rise. There is a view gathering pace that white-collar, permanent jobs are reaching their sell-by dates. For the majority of people, if you want to stay employable, not only will you require cosmetic surgery in the skills department to keep them fresh and desirable, but you must also face up to some deeper changes. These include the way you view your relationship with your employer. Also your job and work practices must adapt to

As Warren G. Bennis puts it "In life, change is inevitable. In business, change is vital."

If you want to stay employable, not only will you require cosmetic surgery in the skills department to keep them fresh and desirable, but you must also face up to some deeper changes.

3

Think about it!

Consider the following real-world, tough questions. Give yourself the time to answer them openly and honestly. If you don't, your employer is probably answering them for you:

- Are you in danger of becoming one of last season's cast-offs?
- Are you fast approaching your sell-by date?
- Are you skills making you a one-hit wonder?
- Are you in decline and in need of an overhaul?
- Are your star qualities fading?
- Are you becoming less attractive or desirable to your boss?

Make an impact every day.

a new working environment. Fortunately, and if you are smart, being an attractive employee can come at an affordable price.

Large, overweight multinationals are regularly reviewing their resources and discarding unwanted staff with clinical efficiency. Such ruthlessness is carried out in the name of survival. The message to employees is simple: add real value or you are out. You need to take decisive action to keep your career marketable and your work prospects high.

These are questions you should ask yourself regularly. Don't become another statistic; instead look at **your vital statistics**: your skills, knowledge and your will to achieve. Show these off! Don't hide your lights. Being modest about how you add value to your organisation will not safeguard your job. You need to fight for your career and keep yourself in your boss's "must have" category. Make an impact every day.

Keep a positive outlook

The state of the economy and, more specifically, the job market provide ample material for many conversations. We hear them on the radio, TV chat shows, in the workplace and at social gatherings. They are almost impossible to avoid. However, most of these "it is not looking good on the job front" conversations bring negative energy into people's lives. Mounting problems are openly discussed. Alarmingly, in these chitchats, the blame for a person's poor current position is usually placed at someone else's door. It is not surprising that blame culture is usually prominent when one is in crisis management mode. As a result, solutions are rarely contemplated but everyone is an expert on what caused the problem. Everyone knows who is to blame and what should have been done to prevent it. Hindsight is wonderful, but it doesn't change your current situation.

The consequence of all this negativity is a self-fulfilling prophecy. Demotivation and the acceptance of their plight engulfs many employees today. There seems to be no way out and all that is left is years of boring, mundane work with an income that just about keeps pace with inflation, or the alternative, which is long-term unemployment. Self-pity blocks creativity and vision.

Now you must stand up, dust yourself off and begin again the work of building your career. It is your life, your career and your happiness. It is time that your career gave you as much excitement and pleasure as your annual holidays or a hobby that you are passionate about. It is time for a **career makeover**. Look in the mirror and see the real you. Bring creativity and energy to the task of remaking your working life. Stay ahead of the latest trends and be a leader rather than a follower when it comes to your career management. It is time for change.

In his Inaugural Address, President Obama talked about the spirit and attitude that is required to start again despite how big the barriers are. "Starting today, we must pick ourselves up, dust ourselves off, and begin again the work of remaking America."

It is time for a career makeover. Look in the mirror and see the real you. Bring creativity and energy to the task of remaking your working life.

What is a career?

Careers are often associated with glamorous or high powered jobs. Modelling careers, sport, film and music careers, and even political careers are labelled as must-have dream jobs, particularly for kids when they are growing up. But what is a career? A simple definition is that your career is how you spend your working life. The *Collins Dictionary* tells us that a career is a "series of jobs in a profession or occupation that a person has through their life". No mention here about high flyers or young ambitious graduates. A career is for everyone, and everyone has a career. As a verb "career" means "rush in an uncontrolled way", which can be a common approach to careers, particularly for those who are slaves to the job market.

People who have considered the type of work that they would like to do are generally more successful and satisfied. They are proactive in seeking out jobs that appeal to them and also allow them to employ the skills that they really enjoy using. Over the years, they have carefully **developed a strategy** to adapt their role to play to their strengths and minimise their shortcomings. They have discovered a meaningful purpose to their career and a balance between doing what they enjoy and keeping the bank manager happy. Very often, they have also managed to get the work/life balance right.

People who have considered the type of work that they would like to do are generally more successful and satisfied.

Managing your career doesn't automatically mean changing the type of job you do, moving to a different department or moving companies. Career strategist John Lees writes that "career management has many dimensions" and that people should look at ways of "discovering the kind of work that [they] find most stimulating and enjoyable". To understand the concept of **career management** it is worth noting some of the possibilities that successful mastery of your career can bring:

- Ensuring that the most productive years of your life are spent doing the type of work that gives you most in terms of fulfilling both your financial and emotional needs.
- Achieving career success as defined by you.
- Developing a role that will energise, excite and encourage you to achieve great things.
- Reaching an acceptable compromise between what you want to do with your career and what the business world has to offer you in terms of work.
- Finding work that you didn't know existed, which makes the most of the skills and knowledge that you enjoy using.
- Achieving the right work/life balance for you, your family and friends.
- Striking a balance between your career and your financial responsibilities.
- Inspiring you to continually grow and develop.

Business and personal management skills

Managing your career effectively, which is about getting the best out of yourself and your talent, requires a comprehensive understanding of fundamental management skills. Learnt skills such as planning, organising and measuring performance have been around since the early days of management theory. Theorists such as Henri Fayol and, later, John Adair, explained that it is the function of managers to set objectives and then have a strategy to achieve them. These overall objectives can be achieved when broken down into smaller more manageable tasks. Once you know what you have to do, a manager's function is then to use all the resources available to ensure these tasks are completed. These proven principles can be adapted and applied to managing your career and your employability.

The skills and techniques that are used throughout this book are the same skills you use on a daily basis to manage your current set of tasks. In addition to the traditional management skills of planning and organising that help you to manage your career successfully, you must also look at ways to strengthen your leadership expertise. Skills such as influencing, decision-making and forward thinking are essential to becoming a master of your career. It is your leadership skills that will help you to create a vision for your future. These tools will make your career work better for you and provide you with the determination and motivation to turn your vision into reality.

You will find some of the skills discussed easy to apply, while other skills will require reworking, practice and persistence. The key to success for top performers is that they are constantly looking at ways to develop and improve. They challenge their performance levels constantly and in doing so they are able to stay on top.

It is time to take responsibility for the success of your career in your chosen profession. After all you own your career and with ownership comes responsibility.

"The price of greatness is responsibility."
Winston Churchill

Building a framework to manage your career

By managing your career, methodically and consciously, you will make it work better for you. To help put a framework on the skills, tools and expertise required to manage your career, consider the **management functions** put forward by French industrialist **Henri Fayol** in the early 1900s and then apply them to your career management strategy. These principles are still relevant and appropriate for today's challenges. Fayol based his theory around the following functions, which can be applied to managing your career:

By managing your career, methodically and consciously, you will make it work better for you.

- **Planning**
  - Setting career goals
  - Budgeting your time and resources spent on building your employability
  - Drawing up a plan of action to achieve these goals

- **Organising**
  - Providing structure to your goals
  - Dividing overall goals into smaller, more manageable tasks
  - Mobilising support from family, friends and colleagues
  - Ensuring that you have the skills and resources to complete each task

- **Commanding**
  - Delegating some activities or task to family, friends and colleagues
  - Giving instructions so that each task is completed
  - Motivating yourself and your support team

- **Co-ordinating**
  - Review all the work that is taking place and amend your plan if necessary
  - Reconcile any differences in your research material, contact details or any other useful information received
  - Ensure that both you and anyone who is helping you with managing your career are working towards a common goal

- **Controlling**
  - Put a measuring/monitoring system in place
  - Measure your results and compare with your original plan
  - Outline your expectation levels
  - Benchmark your performance against your competitors

- **Forecasting**
  - o Examine future opportunities for your skills and knowledge
  - o Research trends in the job market
  - o Define what you have to offer to meet expected demand

Fayol's system of management functions is very much task-oriented. It establishes what has to be done. The next part of the equation is to include in your framework how to get it done. This is the people side of your skills set. Sitting alongside Fayol's management functions in the model below are leaderships skills. Your leadership skills play an important role, as they help you to bring passion, enthusiasm and commitment to your career management strategy. The skills of strategic thinking, decision-making, communicating and inspiring will help you to maintain your focus on achieving results. Combining proven managerial skills with leadership ability skills will provide you with a blueprint for success. Deploy a little work and practice and then all of these skills and tools can be mastered by you.

You own your career

A major advantage in owning your own career is that you can decide what to do with it and the direction it should take. You set the parameters for measuring its success and the satisfaction it brings you. Never live your career through other people – it rarely brings true happiness.

Success means different things to different people. For some people a successful career is about going all the way to the top of the corporate ladder. Such people have the ability and desire to focus on this single career goal, sometimes to the exclusion of everything else. Getting to the top is their mission in life; it's the only thing that truly matters to them. They measure success in terms of power, money and job titles. They thrive on the responsibilities that are associated with senior positions. The bigger the responsibilities, the taller they stand.

"I have always found that my view of success has been iconoclastic: success to me is not about money or status or fame; it's about finding a livelihood that brings me joy and self-sufficiency and a sense of contributing to the world."
Anita Roddick, founder of The Body Shop

Success means different things to different people.

Management	Leadership	Comment
Planning	Strategic thinking	Determining the key goals for your career path: • How you add value in your workplace • Future needs of your customer/employer • Planning your career path • Outlining the direction of your career
Organising	Decision-making	Deciding on which career is best for you: • Understanding the needs of your boss and organisation • Bridging the gap between the work you like and what's on offer • Who can help you • Conducting a skills audit
Commanding	Communicating	To stay in charge of your career progress, you need to manage yourself and your career: • Building your personal brand • Influencing key people • Knowing your unique selling assets • Keeping yourself motivated
Co-ordinating	Inspiring	Bring it all together and remain focused and persistent • Aligning your plan with your vision • Displaying your Personal Vision Statement • Using the 24-hour rule – let's get started now
Controlling	Discipline	Receiving feedback on your performance, potential and value • Making the best use of your performance reviews • Writing your personal development strategy • Focusing on what you can control • Maintaining your persistence
Forecasting	Visionary	Looking beyond the current market requirements • Focusing on your desired position • Capturing all future career opportunities • Identifying career blockages • Researching the job market

Alternatively, career success can also be found in the job itself, in the nature of the work involved. For some people their job is their vocation, and the trappings associated with their chosen career are secondary to the joy that the work itself brings them. They get their energy and rewards from performing their job.

Others simply like to stay doing what they are doing: same work load, and same responsibilities. They are happy and satisfied with their present career and are not looking to climb the corporate ladder. For them their current position is like an old reliable coat, comfortable and safe. Their job is simply a vehicle to pay for their lifestyle. They work to live, rather than live to work.

So, don't confuse high-powered career ambition with having a successful career. This book is about achieving what you consider to be success in your career and personal life. *You* decide what makes your career attractive and fun. Your career is the foundation of your business empire and personal management is the tool you use to ensure its long-term success.

This book is about achieving what you consider to be success in your career and personal life.

Lose the employee mindset, fast!

If the corporate response to the challenges of the 21st Century workplace is to become a lean, flexible and high perform-ing organisation, then it is fair to assume employees need to step up to the mark or run the risk of being ditched. Unfortunately, employers view employees as a cost, and one that they would like to reduce. The competition for jobs has intensified, so one of the ways to compete is to be proactive. Show your employer that what you offer in terms of per-formance and flexibility is what they need, both today and in the future. Surpass their expectations; supply them with outstanding service and productivity every day.

To achieve this level of performance on a consistent basis you must lose your employee mindset as it will restrict your performance and ability to exceed expectations. It will also limit your ability to develop your career and your future employability. An employee mindset is formed over time,

Lose your employee mindset

and for the most part the employee doesn't even realise that they have become a victim of this restrictive condition.

An "**employee mindset**" involves one or more of the following behaviours:

- **You view yourself as just an employee**. You go to work with the attitude that a job is just a job, nothing more nothing less. You give nothing of yourself to the job. You have no emotional attachment to the job.
- **Doing just enough**. Everyday you complete your tasks to a satisfactory level. You do just enough to warrant no negative feedback from management. You have settled for a mediocre-to-good performance level.
- **Having an attitude that your employer owes you a living**. You take your wages every week without stopping to consider if you earned them. The world owes you a living.
- **Confusing years of service with experience**. You believe loyalty deserves wage increases.
- **Refusing to change**. Although the work environment has changed you refuse to adopt new working practices. You fight change and refuse to co-operate. You seek compensation to make changes, even if the changes help you to perform your duties better and easier.
- **9 to 5 mentality**. You leave work even if there are still important and urgent tasks to be completed.
- **Lack of initiative**. You attend meetings but you don't bring any suggestions or input to the table. You demonstrate no initiative when dealing with problems. You expect others to come up with the ideas.
- **Indifference**. You display no drive or enthusiasm for your work. You seldom look to help others but are willing to take any help being offered.
- **"Not in my job description"**. You show no flexibility, if it is not in your job description you don't do it. You suffer from the "silo effect". You never volunteer for any additional tasks.
- **Not needing to learn anything more or anything new**. You reach an impasse when it comes to learning. You don't see the need to up-skill yourself any more or to embrace new techniques.

It's your business

Regardless of whether you view yourself as just an employee or that you have developed a serious employee mindset, you must take action to change this attitude. It is important that you shift your way of thinking from that of being an employee to that of being an entrepreneur. **Seeing yourself as a business that provides a service is the first critical step you must take in order to become a marketable and employable package and set yourself apart from the crowd.**

It is important to stress that it is not any old boring company that you will create: it is time for you to become "I Add Value Ltd" and start to build your business empire around delivering extraordinary results. Entrepreneurs actively seek out ways to improve things, such as work practices, new products, and cost efficiencies. In the 21st Century workplace people will be expected to meet these challenges and service the needs of their employer.

Personal management, or management of yourself, is the business space that your company operates in and its main focus is on managing your career and the service that you provide. Managing your career is about more than simply doing your job. It is about how you look and behave, your skills and expertise, as well as your level of performance. An understanding of the constant changing expectation levels of your boss is paramount to your survival. You will need to develop all the business acumen that is required to run a successful company. You will manage yourself, your career and those around you with all the skill of a successful entrepreneur.

Become "I Add Value Ltd" and start to build your business empire around delivering extraordinary results

"I never perfected an invention that I did not think about in terms of the service it might give others… I find out what the world needs, then I proceed to invent."

Thomas Edison

Every business has its departments

Managing yourself in the same way that you would manage a company allows you to take a corporate approach to your career. Successful companies are made up of several different departments such as sales, marketing, production, etc. According to Michael Porter's "Value Chain", each of these departments must add value to the business if it wants to be profitable. Your company (I Add Value Ltd) is also made up of several departments:

Customer Service:	The skills, knowledge and expertise that you provide and that your employer pays for
Research & Development	Up-skilling yourself to keep pace with your employer's current and future needs
Marketing	Personal branding, your unique selling point (USP), and how you sell yourself
Quality assurance	Performance reviews and regular feedback

If you are to be successful, consider that each of your departments is dependent on the others for its success. Bob Hartley and Michael W. Starkey write in their book *The Management of Sales and Customer Relations* that departments "all need to work together to satisfy customers' needs". Each of the above departments, and more, will be discussed throughout this book to build a focused strategy designed to ensure that you give yourself the best chance of being a master of your career.

Who are your customers?

The main focus of any business is to create customers, and you are no different. However, in your business model, your employer becomes your primary customer. This approach fundamentally changes your working relationships. You no longer have the traditional employee/employer relationship with your job or your boss. You are not just an employee, who works standard hours with the sole purpose of picking up your wage at the end of the week for completing the same tasks over and over again. 21st Century workers need to focus on their customer's/employer's changing requirements. Changing your relationship from employer/employee to customer/service provider will accelerate the process of

The main focus of any business is to create customers, and you are no different.

establishing what your employer truly values and expects from you.

Keeping your customer/employer or customers/employers happy is vital to your business success and future employment. Understanding their needs is the foundation for building a competitive strategy that will differentiate you from your colleagues. Consistently meeting and then exceeding those needs will ensure your employability.

Being a good employee will no longer guarantee your job. Customers/employers demand more.

Changing your relationship from employer/employee to customer/service provider will accelerate the process of establishing what your employer truly values and expects from you.

A planned approach to career management

Your business plan should be developed around conducting regular business needs analysis. The plan will incorporate an effective personal branding strategy, together with clear understanding of your unique selling point(s) so that you will stand out in a positive way from colleagues. It will also develop a framework that will promote innovative ways to consistently add value to your customer/employer and provide an emphasis on a strategic plan for your future development. This, in turn, will enhance your reputation, making you more marketable. Being in business isn't easy, as there are no quick fixes; but the rewards can be very satisfying.

Another advantage of operating "as a business" is that it allows you to become more impartial and less emotionally involved when dealing with critical career management issues. You can ask yourself more difficult and important questions such as:

Operating "as a business" allows you to become more impartial and less emotionally involved when dealing with critical career management issues.

- Does my current role have a future?
- Will my skills become obsolete in the future?
- Is my loyalty misplaced?
- Am I as flexible as my customer/employer needs?
- Am I getting a fair price for what I deliver?
- Does my current customer/employer have a future?
- How long will my **Unique Selling Point** (USP) remain unique?

Have you mortgaged your career on the success of this one employer?

A feature of successful companies is their ability to ensure that they have diversified, sustainable revenue streams that are not over-reliant on one customer.

If you only have one source of income and it unexpectedly goes bust, then there is the distinct possibility you could too.

Some of the answers to these questions can leave you very exposed. For instance, how many customers do you actually have? For most people the answer is "**one**": your current employer. If this is the case, does your single source of income cover your outgoings? How secure is this sole source of revenue? What would happen to you if you lost this customer through redundancy or for some other reason outside your control? Have you mortgaged your career on the success of this one employer?

Going bust

A feature of successful companies is their ability to ensure that they have diversified, sustainable revenue streams that are not over-reliant on one customer. As an employee, your current business model is at risk of being over-dependent on one customer – your employer. In uncertain times, this characteristic of the traditional employer/employee relationship seriously threatens your survival. If you only have one source of income and it unexpectedly goes bust, then there is the distinct possibility you could too. This is a fundamental economic reality currently facing millions of people throughout Europe and North America. It is highly unlikely that any other type of company would put themselves in such a risky and, some corporate analysts would say, reckless position.

Nevertheless, this is the out-of-date working practice that the vast majority of people have accepted. You have one job, which equals one customer – one source of income. In a rapidly changing and unpredictable business world, this could have disastrous results. You need to start thinking about how you can reduce the effect this over-dependence has on your economic welfare. Arguably, it is prudent to embark on a restructuring programme to increase your revenue stream and some of these options will be discussed later in the book. However, some initial ways of improving your income can be achieved by either charging more for your services, for example securing a wage increase through promotion, or by increasing your customer base by taking on some additional part-time work in the evenings or weekends. Whatever route you decide to embark on, it is imperative that you start the process immediately.

Begin the process of viewing yourself as a business by asking yourself these simple but challenging questions. Be honest and thoughtful in your answers.

These are the sort of questions you should be asking yourself today, not when you find yourself unemployed. Unfortunately, most people wait until they are vulnerable (out of a job) before asking themselves these important career-enhancing questions. When you are at a low point you rarely think clearly, so naturally your answers may miss or ignore key areas. Stay ahead of the crowd and become a business leader, not follower. Conduct your review when you are in a positive frame of mind.

Develop a bank of questions for yourself that will keep you focused on building your career. Get into the habit of answering these questions when you are in a strong and confident mood. As a result, your answers should help you with your business plan. If you build your business empire with a meaningful skills portfolio and from a position of strength, it will be robust.

Your customer/employer is king

If you are reliant on just one customer or employer, how well do you treat your most important source of revenue? Have you crowned your customer/employer king? Are you always trying to please your customer/employer? Do you make a conscious decision every day to give value for money? British writer Nelson Boswell follows a simple principle: "always give people more than they expect to get", and that way you will keep your competitors at bay.

Learn to love your customer/employer before someone else does. If you are not romancing or showing your appreciation of your customer/employer on a regular basis, the chances are they may look elsewhere. Taking someone for granted can happen in any relationship and over time this can lead to a break-up which is usually avoidable.

"Anything worth doing is worth doing now!"

Ralph Stayer
(American Businessman)

Think about it!

Your answers need to be given with total honesty and the cold air of reality so that you will have a clear picture of your employability status.

✓ If you were to lose your job in the morning, how would it affect you?
✓ What level of income would you be left with?
✓ Would you easily get a replacement job?
✓ Are your skills transferable?
✓ How easy is it to market yourself?
✓ Do you have a contingency plan in place?
✓ Do you know what jobs are available at the moment?
✓ What savings do you have?
✓ Can you relocate easily to find suitable work?

If you are reliant on just one customer or employer, how well do you treat your most important source of revenue?

Learn to love your customer/employer before someone else does.

Relationships by their nature require constant care and attention. Your customer/employer needs reminding every so often that you really appreciate their custom.

Entrepreneur mindset vs employee mindset

Think about it!

Are you what a customer/employer views as stylish or out of style?

Stylish: Entrepreneur Mindset	Out of style: Employee Mindset
I'm passionate about my clients	I do my job well
I take pride in my appearance	Sure I'm fine the way I am
I'm determined to excel at my job	I'm happy that I'm good at what I do
I earn my wages and give value for money	They should pay me more for what I do
I love to smile and bring energy to my workplace	First thing I do is smile, to get it over with
I love to wear bright colours	I wear grey, that way I won't stand out

Thriving companies carry out regular reviews of their business to ensure continued success. They are constantly updating their image and operations to guarantee existing customer satisfaction and to attract new business.

Have a makeover

Thriving companies carry out regular reviews of their business to ensure continued success. They are constantly updating their image and operations to guarantee existing customer satisfaction and to attract new business. They fear complacency. If they stand still they will be overtaken by their competitors. It is wise to periodically check out the competition and assess where you stand.

Put some time aside in the near future to carry out your review and update your image and business model. The results of this exercise will form the basis of your makeover. Your transformation will include outlining your personal vision, assessing your skills and carrying out a comprehensive business needs analysis. It also includes ditching any employee mindset characteristics you may have. This makeover will help you formulate your strategic plan for the future.

Undergoing the most important makeover of your career will transform you into a magnet for business opportunities. It will be fun and you will discover many assets you didn't realise you had or controlled. You will receive positive affirmation from your customer/employer and colleagues when you launch your new business model.

What's your personal vision?

You can develop a vision for your life by using the same skills that you have used in your working environment. Always start with a clear understanding of the end result. Articulate your dreams by simply writing them down on a page. Include how you will feel when you are spending your time doing the job that you want to do. Then ask yourself a few simple questions to establish how you will get there. Suddenly, the obstacles that were preventing you from living your life the way you wanted to live it are no longer insurmountable.

Once you have articulated your goals, which are your blueprint for success, then make a commitment to yourself to complete them. Don't waste any more time looking for excuses to prevent you from achieving your dreams. In most cases, there is nothing stopping you, other than yourself. You can make it easier for yourself by telling someone close to you, someone who will support you, about your new commitments. Seek their encouragement if you have any doubts.

Your new business venture of career management must

Put some time aside in the near future to carry out your review and update your image and business model.

"Obstacles are those frightful things you see when you take your eyes off your goal."
Henry Ford

Once you have articulated your goals, then make a commitment to yourself to complete them.

have a **personal vision statement**. Your vision should articulate where you are guiding your business to and its primary purpose. It is a view of your future and the strategic choices you need to make along the way. Your personal vision is what you want to achieve and how you would like to see it happen. It provides you with a sense of direction. As top motivational speaker Anthony Robbins puts it:

"There is a powerful driving force inside every human being that once unleashed can make any vision, dream, or desire a reality."
Anthony Robbins

> "There is a powerful driving force inside every human being that once unleashed can make any vision, dream, or desire a reality."

You should also know how and when to transform your business in an ever-changing and competitive corporate environment. Your vision must allow you to adapt to change in a way that delivers real and sustainable value for your customer/employer. You can't avoid change – you must embrace it. Use change to your advantage.

You can't avoid change – you must embrace it. Use change to your advantage.

Creating a personal vision statement is challenging; for probably the first time you are committing to paper what you would like to achieve. Some questions might enter your mind such as: "am I being ambitious enough" or "am I being over ambitious"? "What happens if my vision doesn't become a reality?" You can overcome these doubts by ensuring that your personal vision statement has a comprehensive understanding of both your assets and your customer's/employer's desires. Having the capabilities to nurture this understanding will make your business strong and vigorous and ready to deal with any change.

For probably the first time you are committing to paper what you would like to achieve.

It is this type of thinking and foresight that is needed in today's tough business environment. It will help you improve your competitiveness and marketability. Your unique personal vision will set you apart from the crowd.

Your unique personal vision will set you apart from the crowd.

Live your vision

Your vision is your blueprint for success, so you need to live it. Bring your vision to life. Everyday complete some task, however small, that will turn your vision into reality. This

Everyday complete some task, however small, that will turn your vision into reality.

will help you to remain focused on the purpose, strategy and values of you as your business. In short, your vision is about why you exist, what you do, how you do it and what you believe to be important. It is your roadmap to sustainable employment.

Your vision statement

It is important that you write down your vision in a *Personal Vision Statement*. This will bring clarity to your business. Display it where you can view it every day. Keep it concise, but challenging and ambitious. Show it to key people and get their feedback. Your Personal Vision Statement is what your business stands for, what you stand for. It is what you believe you will provide your customer/employer with, both consistently and honestly.

Your Personal Vision Statement states your business purpose and reason for existence. It is this unique vision that will give your customers/employers satisfaction, and as a result you should win repeat business, the sort of business that you want, and which means that you are meeting your customers'/employers' requirements.

Review and update your Personal Vision Statement as your situation and circumstances change. Keep it fresh and exciting. Live your vision with pride and enthusiasm.

Staying on the same page

Once you have created your own "company" to promote your career, you must ensure that the service that you provide is aligned to your customer's/employer's needs and desires. If you are not in tune with the needs of your customer/employer, then this can lead to frustration and career disappointments, and your hard work will go unrewarded.

Personal Vision Statement: An Example of What it Could Be

To remain employable I have to establish a vision with clear goals. The following guiding principles will help me measure my success:

1. Apply the highest standard of excellence to my job
2. Contribute to creating a great work environment and treat my customer/employer and colleagues with respect and dignity
3. Continuously seek ways to add value to my customer/employer
4. Recognise that profitability is essential to the success of my customer/employer and my future employment
5. Update my skills, knowledge and tools so that I'm at the cutting edge of my profession
6. Build mutual loyalty with my customer/employer

When was the last time you did this?

✓ Talked to your customer/employer and found out what their real needs are and how you can meet these.
✓ Asked your customer/employer to complete a personalised customer satisfaction questionnaire.
✓ Discussed their future plans and how you might fit into them.

Are you a slave to your job?

You can become a slave to your job without realising it. You don't set out to become a slave. You don't wake up one Monday morning and decide that you want to be a slave. Most people start their working lives full of hope, ambition and enthusiasm. Somehow, over time, slave-like behaviour just creeps up on them and ultimately traps them. The slave mentality gains control over a period of time and they display the symptoms, but fail to recognise or acknowledge them.

This slave-like mindset and behaviour is often easier to spot in other people than to recognise in one's own life. As a result there are many people suffering the effects of such behaviour who are unable to break free.

Take a risk

"Entrepreneurs are risk takers, willing to roll the dice with their money or reputation on the line in support of an idea or enterprise. They willingly assume responsibility for the success or failure of a venture and are answerable for all its facets."

Victor Kiam

To become a master of your career you need to develop the mindset of a successful entrepreneur. You need creativity, a real desire for success and to take responsibility for your performance.

This is your career; you and you alone are responsible for its success or failure. Displaying the right attitude greatly enhances your chances of being a true master of your career and in so doing ensures your employability.

The entrepreneurial spirit is often suppressed by people's bosses, who would rather work by the "we always do it this way" principle; or hampered by well-meaning family and friends who have limited vision and live by the "don't dream too big or you might have a big fall" principle. Taking control of building your career will often involve some element of risk as you break free from your comfort zone. A creative imagination will give you the platform to seek out the opportunities that others don't see.

Ask and answer the hard questions posed to see if you are a slave to your job or master of your career. Pick up the tools discussed in the book, and look at how you can use them to ensure your employability.

Some of the tools and techniques discussed in this book will work for you – others won't. You need to personalise this entire book so that it will enhance your vision and enable you to work your plan like a real visionary. Ask and answer the hard questions posed to see if you are a slave to your job or master of your career. Pick up the tools discussed in the book, even if you have tried them before, and look at how you can use them to ensure your employability. Take control and responsibility for your career. Don't be discouraged by other people just because it didn't work for them. Persistence and dedication to excellence will bring improvement, not overnight but over time. There are risks associated with change, but equally there are risks attached to ignoring the need to change.

Benefits of being a Master of your Career

Your career is important to you as it can satisfy both your financial and emotional needs. Managing your career requires an investment of your time, commitment to change and the capacity to be a visionary. The time that you invest in writing and implementing your Personal Vision Statement and your Personal Business Plan, which we will discuss later, will pay off in an overall improvement of your life, both in work and at home. There are many advantages to being a Master of your Career:

- You bring energy and enthusiasm to your work.
- You are seen in a positive light by both your colleagues and bosses.
- You improve your work/life balance.
- You do the work that excites you.
- You have the mindset to overcome any obstacles.
- You are more likely to be headhunted for the best roles.
- You will build your profile to ensure your future employability status.

> **You know you are a Master of your Career when:**
>
> - You clearly understand what success means for you
> - You genuinely enjoy going to work
> - You get a buzz from the work you do
> - You have endless energy and enthusiasm
> - You understand the needs of your customer/employer
> - You deliver on those needs
> - You are a high performer
> - You make a positive impact
> - You are employable

Managing your career requires an investment of your time, commitment to change and the capacity to be a visionary.

Do's and Don'ts of Managing your Career

DO:

- ✓ **Be a Master**
- ✓ Think, act and behave like an entrepreneur.
- ✓ Manage your career using sound and proven management principles.
- ✓ Treat your employer as your Number 1 Customer.
- ✓ Move from crisis management to strategic management.
- ✓ Analyse your vital statistics – your skills, knowledge and your will to achieve.
- ✓ Assume responsibility for the success of your career.
- ✓ Decide what makes your career attractive and fun.
- ✓ Build your business empire around delivering extraordinary results.

DON'T:

- ☒ **Don't Be a Slave**
- ☒ Don't look in the mirror and see yourself as an employee.
- ☒ Don't believe that a career is for other people.
- ☒ Don't wait until you are ditched before helping yourself and your career.
- ☒ Don't think that it will never happen to you.
- ☒ Don't be trapped in an employee mindset.
- ☒ Don't refuse to update your image and business operations.
- ☒ Don't rush around working hard in a directionless way.
- ☒ Don't be over-reliant on one source of income.
- ☒ Don't stand still and allow competitors to upstage you.
- ☒ Don't waste too much time and energy talking about the past and feeling sorry for yourself.

Before you read any further, take a break and write down the first part of your plan to ensure your employability.

PERSONAL THOUGHTS

What will I do differently tomorrow?

CHAPTER 2
PLANNING:
YOUR BUSINESS PLAN TO KEEP WORKING

Quick guide to this chapter

- You need to plan
- Mapping the route
- Your career vision
- Create your storyboard
- Developing a Business Plan for your career:
  The Virgin Land Approach
- What's in your Business Plan
- Building a vision for your future employment

We tend to spend more time planning our annual holiday than planning our careers. Why is this? Forgetting to plan your holiday or leaving it to luck just simply wouldn't be an option for most people because it could go horribly wrong, with massive disappointment for all concerned, together with the inevitable financial implications. You would never walk into a travel agent and expect them to know what you are looking for in a holiday or that they should be required to organise your dream holiday with little or no information about your needs or preferences. Experience has taught you that planning is a forerunner to success. Therefore, before visiting your travel agent you would have a good idea of what

We tend to spend more time planning our annual holiday than planning our careers.

you are looking for, completed the necessary research and narrowed down your destination of choice to a few preferred options. As a result, it is no surprise then that most people enjoy a wonderful, relaxing holiday.

If this logical approach to ensuring that we have an enjoyable holiday works for most of us, then why do we spend more time planning our annual holiday than planning our career? A career lasts a lifetime of 45 years or more, but a holiday only lasts two weeks. So why is there such a disparity in the time that you spend in planning them? Isn't your career a more important element of your overall happiness? Indeed, without a career could you afford to go on holiday?

What causes such irrational behaviour in intelligent people? Could Scott Adams, the author of the incredibly popular "Dilbert" cartoon strip, be correct when he proposes his theory behind the bizarre workplace behaviours that inhabit the corporate world? "People are idiots", he explains. Is this the reason why people refuse to plan their careers?

"People are idiots." Is this the reason why people refuse to plan their careers?

Perhaps "idiots" is too strong, and perhaps there are other more sophisticated reasons to explain this remarkable imbalance between holiday and career planning. It may be kinder and more palatable to say that most people fail to plan their career because they think along the following lines:

- I'm lucky to have my job in today's climate
- Careers are more for high flyers
- I don't see the need
- I haven't got the time
- I enjoy what I do
- My career is moving along steadily

An additional excuse for the lack of time being devoted to career planning is that it may not be a priority for most people. Holidays are more pressing and there will always be time to develop a career. However, procrastination in career planning is not recommended. You can always book another holiday, but a career opportunity may not come as fast again.

"Don't wait. The time will never be just right."

Napoleon Hill

Although excuses given for postponing career planning are self-explanatory, it is worth discussing them a little further. Always remember that it is your career, your life, your happiness and your success that you are planning. It is in your interest to have a fulfilling career, not just your employer's interest.

Always remember that it is your career, your life, your happiness and your success that you are planning. It is in your interest to have a fulfilling career, not just your employer's interest.

"In today's economic climate, I'm lucky to have my job"

In today's turbulent working environment, it is becoming a widely held view that there is no sense in building a career as there are no new jobs or promotional opportunities available; that as companies are cutting back aggressively, you might be putting yourself at risk by switching jobs; and that you are safer staying where you are.

However, though the jobs market is slow, it is imperative that you plan for the upturn. You must be ready to take advantage of the opportunities when they arrive. Waiting until the market improves means that you will be at a disadvantage and a number of steps behind those who do plan their careers.

Plan for the upturn.

It is also very important that you start the process of career planning today in order to hold on to your current job. Don't be naïve in thinking that just because you have a job now you don't have to think about your future employ-ability. Build a strategy that will ensure that your job isn't the one that is cut. Your current role and the way in which you perform in it must add value to your employer/customer.

Start the process of career planning today in order to hold on to your current job.

"Careers are for high flyers"

Careers are often associated solely with people whose aim in life is to reach the top of the corporate ladder; with people who are ambitious and focused in their pursuit of career advancement. However, careers are for everyone. "Career" is simply a word to describe your working life. Taking a narrow view of what a career means will reduce your opportunities. Although a high-flying career gets more attention, everyone needs to have a sense of where they are going in order to

Careers are for everyone.

If you don't plan your career, someone else will and you might not like the results.

ensure that their career remains viable. Also, if you don't plan your career, someone else will and you might not like the results.

"I don't see the need for career planning"

Some people are content to amble their way through life. They enjoy their job and their easy way of life. They don't see the need to plan for the future; they live life in the moment. Although this philosophy has its merits, there are also risks attached to it. The current global changes taking place in working methods will impact on everyone to some degree. The traditional 9 to 5, pensionable job is being steadily replaced by more flexible working patterns.

Assuming or hoping that these changes will not affect you is not an advisable strategy. Now is not the time to bury your head in the sand and hope that things will remain as they have been. Employ the process of career planning to investigate ways of maintaining your lifestyle while adjusting to new work practices. Keep at least one step ahead of the inevitable changes.

"I haven't got the time to plan"

You often hear people say "I'm too busy working and getting things done to have time to plan my career". The truth is everyone has time to plan their career, and an investment in planning will save time and stress in the long-term. Most people feel that they don't have sufficient time for planning until something drastic happens, such as redundancy. If you are too busy to plan your career because of your current work commitment, then you will develop a narrow focus. You will miss opportunities and become too slow to react to threats to your career and employability.

If you are too busy to plan your career because of your current work commitment. You will miss opportunities and become too slow to react to threats to your career and employability.

(If time management is an issue for you then it is time to read my book *Slave to the Clock, Master of Time* and develop a strategy that will incorporate your career plans. You need to change your behaviour and invest some time in planning your career. Otherwise you may end up with more free time than you would like.)

"I enjoy what I do"

Maybe you have found the best job in the world and you love what you do. You are highly motivated and a top performer. Your boss loves you, which is reflected in your salary and big bonus each year. However, John Lees in his book *How to Get a Job You'll Love* writes

> "There are dangers here, too: your work/life balance may need adjustments. Perhaps work plays too important a part in your life. Those who suffer the greatest impact of redundancy are those who have made their work the most important thing in their life, perhaps at the expense of family or personal development."

"Those who suffer the greatest impact of redundancy are those who have made their work the most important thing in their life, perhaps at the expense of family or personal development."

John Lees

The fact that you enjoy your current job doesn't exclude you from planning your career. You may also be excellent at what you do, but there are no guaranteed jobs – every job has a certain degree of risk. Part of any robust plan would include some reflection on the following:

- Can you keep up your current high level of performance?
- Will this job still be required in the medium to long term?
- Are you adapting to changing workplace models?
- What's your strategy to ensure that you do not become complacent and stale?

"My career is moving along steadily"

Another reason why some of you spend little time planning your career is that to date it has progressed as you would have liked. You got your qualification, you are involved in lots of interesting work and projects, and you may have even

Has your career progressed due to circumstances rather than by choice?

landed a promotion. However, the jobs market has changed significantly. Has your career progressed due to circumstances rather than by choice? For instance, have you been the beneficiary of people leaving your organisation and, therefore, allowing interesting work to become available? Was there real competition for the promotion? You need to reflect honestly on the reasons why your career has progressed so well to date and whether you can maintain its future growth.

"It is easy to follow, but it is uninteresting to do easy things. We find out about ourselves only when we take risks, when we challenge and question."
Magdalena Abakanowicz (Polish Sculptor)

If you are one of the countless people who spend more time planning their holidays than planning their career: stop! It is now time to change your way of thinking and give your career the prominence that it requires. This change will become the bedrock of your long-term happiness.

Mapping the route

When you embark on a long and arduous journey, to a place where you have never been, you will probably plan your route thoroughly. You might purchase a map outlining the various routes to take. Alternatively, you might ask for detailed instructions of how to get there from an experienced and trusted traveller. However, a note of caution: when you talk to experts, there is no point asking questions that give answers to things you already know and, in doing so, failing to get the answers that you need. Think carefully about the type of questions you must ask in order to plan your journey correctly.

Start the process of career planning by asking some simple initial questions such as "Do you know where you want your career to go?" or "Do you know how to get there?" The real purpose of planning is to make sure you are not misled into falsely believing you know something that you don't actually know. Robert M. Pirsig in his book, *Zen and the Art of Motorcycle Maintenance*, points out:

> "This careful approach to the beginning questions keeps you from taking a major wrong turn which might cause you weeks of extra work or can even hang you up completely. Scientific questions often have a surface

appearance of dumbness for this reason. They are asked in order to prevent dumb mistakes later on."

When it comes to your career the only "dumb" questions are the ones that are not asked. It is amazing how frequently the obvious question is never asked until it is often too late and a golden career opportunity is missed.

When going on new journeys, most of us plan, because we like to know where we are going and don't want any unexpected or nasty surprises. We have an inherent fear of the unknown. Once we know how to reach our destination, our anxiety levels drop and we enjoy the trip.

Careers are often journeys into the unknown but with adequate planning we can reduce some of our anxieties and fears. Learning a new skill after many years, being promoted out of a comfort zone, or finding a new job after redundancy are the types of journeys that are being undertaken by people in today's job market. For many, it is a new road. This can be a daunting journey, especially if you are not prepared. It will be a long road with many potholes, twists and turns. It is vital that you plan your journey in order to improve your chances of reaching your desired destination.

In business, profitable and innovative companies have short-, medium- and long-term plans. Managers of such businesses like to plan, as planning provides a degree of security and a greater understanding of how objectives will be achieved. Their plans are results-driven, blueprints for continuous achievement. Managers of successful businesses set challenging targets and go about reaching them with energy and enthusiasm. Milestones are agreed to monitor their progress. Planning is their road map to success.

The same business approach is required to build a strategy to keep your current job or find a new one when required. As with all profitable companies you should have short-, medium- and long-term plans. This applies to everyone, irrespective of whether you are currently happy with your job or find yourself unemployed. These plans form a central part of your vision for the future and your marketability. Careful preparation now and investment of your time in planning will provide you with a rich harvest of opportunities in future years.

> When it comes to your career the only "dumb" questions are the ones that are not asked. It is amazing how frequently the obvious question is never asked until it is often too late and a golden career opportunity is missed.

> "To accomplish great things, we must not only act, but also dream; not only plan, but also believe."
> Anatole France, French poet and Nobel laureate

> As with all profitable companies you should have short-, medium- and long-term plans.

Building a vision for your future employment

Transfer the principles of planning into the business of running your career and you will start to appreciate the similarities. All successful business plans start by looking to the future. Don't waste time dwelling on the past, whether you were successful or had bad experiences. What's done is done, and you cannot change it, but you can influence your future and your future employment possibilities. Learn from past experiences, both positive and negative. It is important that mistakes are not replicated and that successes are built upon.

To survive in the jobs market you need to be able to anticipate the rapidly changing needs of your employer/customer and then have the drive to reinvent yourself to meet these needs. People who enjoy continuous success in finding work build strategies that can be easily adapted to their changing environment. Their strategies are based around creating a vision that incorporates the things that they need to keep and the areas that they need to change. Developing a framework to create a vision will help to eliminate vague or woolly concepts that are often high on aspiration but bear no resemblance to reality and, consequently, are rarely achieved. Great visionaries have the ability to convert their vision into reality.

Writing your personal vision statement is the first step in developing your business plan. A personal vision statement, as discussed in **Chapter 1**, is your view of how you would like your business life to turn out. It tells you where you are going and it gives you a sense of direction and purpose. Your vision statement should be ambitious; it should stretch you and also inspire you.

"The only limits are, as always, those of vision."

James Broughton, American poet

In Chapter 1 we looked at writing a personal vision statement as a statement of intent. This outlined the direction in which your career was going. The next step is to plan how to turn your vision into reality. The framework outlined here for developing your vision statement will bring clarity to your future employability.

A good place to start is by establishing what you want

from your career. Review your personal vision statement from Chapter 1. Then talk (or "**brainstorm**") with some friends or family members to generate more ideas about what you like to do, what skills you enjoy using and what type of work brings you enjoyment and fulfilment. Keep the discussion as broad as possible because, as the Nobel Prize-winning chemist, Linus Pauling, explained:

"The best way to have a good idea is to have lots of ideas."

Ask questions, such as what strengths of yours have other people commented on, what new areas of work would you like to explore? You may have an idea of what you want from your career already, but don't let that stop you from exploring other options. Write down as many ideas as possible. Be creative and remain open-minded. At this stage, don't question any of the ideas that are generated. Sometimes it is the idea that sounded weird or outlandish initially that turns out to be the best initiative.

Once you have exhausted all of your ideas, start the second brainstorming session – the **customer/employer analysis**. Review your current customer's/employer's requirements. Where are the opportunities and strengths in your career? Can you be replaced easily? What skills does your customer/employer deem to be the most valuable? Look externally also. Make a list of what business sectors are employing people at present, or are likely to employ people in the future. What are the growth areas? Who are the market leaders and innovators? What sectors are in a stable environment? This may need some additional research to gather information and generate a comprehensive list. Don't overlook or dismiss any job possibilities at this stage. You need to understand the **full** jobs market.

Make a list of what business sectors are employing people at present, or are likely to employ people in the future.

When you have completed the customer/employer analysis you then need to list the type of jobs that are available in these areas. Find out the job and person specifications for each position. As these employers are potential future customers of yours, you should pay careful attention to the skills and competencies that they are looking for. This will help you to build a profile of the future work landscape.

At this stage of the process you have constructed **two detailed lists outlining your skills preferences and what type of jobs are on offer**. These lists will be used again when you develop your business plan. The next part of the process is to bridge the gap between what's available and what you would like to work at. This will involve a mixture of elimination and compromise. It will also feed into your personal development plan, because to bridge some of the gaps you may need to do some up-skilling.

to bridge the gap between what's available and what you would like to work at will involve a mixture of elimination and compromise

You are now ready to write an insightful vision statement and map for turning it into reality. This is the "what and how" process: what is your career and how will you get there. Sit alone in a comfortable room and close your eyes. Visualise how you would like your career to turn out. It is now commonplace for top performing sports people to use visualisation as part of their routine in the lead-up to major sporting events. It allows them to focus on their goal and to eliminate any distractions or barriers. They become completely immersed in their quest to achieve their goal. This driven approach gives them the edge in their pursuit of peak performance and, ultimately, success.

Visualise how you would like your career to turn out.

When you are in a relaxed state of mind, and with your eyes closed, begin the process of visualising your future with the end in mind.

When visualising, remember your brainstorming sessions, as during these you painted a clear picture of what you want from your career. Now use words to describe this scene using positive and powerful phrases. Use the present tense, as this will galvanise you into immediate action. Use language that you can relate to as this is your **personal** vision statement, and always write in the first person as it is more powerful when you take responsibility for your career.

Ask yourself some simple questions:

- What type of work am I doing?
- How enjoyable is it?
- How strong financially am I?
- Is the work challenging enough?
- How does this work make me more employable?

The purpose of your vision statement is to motivate, energise and maintain your passion for your career and the work you do. It serves to open up your eyes to the possibilities that are available to you. It is important to think big, aim high and push yourself to accomplish great achievements. Dr Bob Rotella, a renowned sports psychologist and performance coach, talks about achieving great things through thinking big.

Your career ambitions can be as big or as small as you want. The important thing is not to settle for something less than you want. Don't have a career full of regrets and missed opportunities.

Your personal vision statement creates an awareness of what you can achieve. It shows you a picture of what you want to do and can do if the barriers, whether they are perceived or real, are brought down. It brings clarity and a focused understanding of the type of work that you will do. When you are out of work or stuck in a rut, these possibilities and ambitions seem to be out of reach. Make a decision now to create a personal vision statement that will inspire you to greatness, working in a job that you deserve. Anthony Robbins, a world-renowned motivational speaker, believes that: "It is in your moments of decision that your destiny is shaped."

A sample vision statement might look like this:

> "A person with great dreams can achieve great things. A person with small dreams, or a person without the confidence to pursue his or her dreams, has consigned himself or herself to a life of frustration and mediocrity."
>
> Bob Rotella

Personal Vision Statement

I give my customer/employer continuous outstanding work by maintaining my drive to add value to them by exceeding their expectations at every opportunity. I have won Salesperson of the Year for the third time. I constantly strive to improve myself personally and professionally so that I can pursue a successful career that I enjoy and can overcome any challenges that I face. I have just completed a Diploma in Managing People in which my final assignment was voted best in class. I review my skills quarterly to ensure that I remain a market leader in learning and development and the preferred choice of my customer/employer. I have been promoted to Sales Director for Ireland and the UK.

> "It is in your moments of decision that your destiny is shaped."
>
> Anthony Robbins

As mentioned earlier your personal vision statement is a "whats and hows" process. In the sample statement there are three main "whats and hows". For example, the first "what" is continuous outstanding work and the "how" is winning Salesperson of the Year.

Design a storyboard that sells your vision for your employability

a storyboard will help you to organise and focus your story and identify any gaps in your career map

Creating a storyboard is an excellent way to visually represent your personal vision statement and map to success. It is your plan that shows how you intend to become a master of your own destiny by being employable. It will help you to organise and focus your story and identify any gaps in your career map.

Start your storyboard by collecting all of the pieces of your journey; they don't need to be in any order at this stage. This is the creative part, so it is important to refrain from thinking in a linear way. Your storyboard should contain a printed version of your personal vision statement. Write a brief profile of the two main characters in this story, you and your customer/employer. You already have this information from your earlier brainstorming session. Leave some room to add other characters who will play an important role in your story. We will talk further about who can help you later in the book when we discuss networking and mentoring.

Your storyboard should also contain your favourite quotes, which will sustain your motivation and inspire you to implement your business plan. It should be bright and uplifting. It is a fun way to show people that you are serious about changing the way you manage your life.

Then arrange each piece of your storyboard in a logical sequence. As you read through this book, and follow its advice, you will be able to add more pieces to the storyboard and as a result the picture will become clearer. A good storyboard will convey your key message to your target audience and support that message with visual images and snappy texts. Actually seeing a visual image of your career can be a powerful tool in galvanising your efforts to build that career. Once you start implementing your personal vision to be employable you may change things. Update your storyboard with new ideas as your story develops. **Turn your vision into an outstanding business plan**

A good storyboard will convey your key message to your target audience and support that message with visual images and snappy texts. Actually seeing a visual image of your career can be a powerful tool in galvanising your efforts to build that career.

"Vision without action is a daydream. Action without vision is a nightmare."
Japanese proverb

Your storyboard should provide you with a visual overview of your vision for your career. The successful implementation of your vision starts with a good business plan.

Your career plan is a simple document that tells your story by looking to the future and preparing you for opportunities and threats. It outlines your strategy and how you will allocate your resources to achieve your goals. It describes your key strengths and the business sector that you are interested in. Your plan will include a job market analysis and forecast. It should also contain details of your financial position. The elements and characteristics of an outstanding personal business plan are:

- Purpose
- Simplicity
- Flexibility
- Realism
- Written
- Signed

The elements and characteristics of an outstanding personal business plan are:
- Purpose
- Simplicity
- Flexibility
- Realism
- Written
- Signed

Purpose of your plan Before you start the process of writing, you must decide on the exact purpose of your plan. What exactly are you trying to achieve? What will it help you to do? What are you trying to get from it?

Establishing the rationale behind your plan will give you a direction and focus. It will help you to concentrate on some tangible results. Think about the end result, your personal vision and what you will be doing once your plan has been successfully implemented. At this stage don't concern yourself too much with how you will get there, just focus on the purpose of your career plan.

KISS – Keep it Simple Stupid 'KISS' your way to success. Although this formula sounds easy, it can be challenging to keep it short and concise. It may require numerous drafts before you have the right plan, and you will need to ensure it communicates your ideas and objectives in a practical way. When you are out of a job or planning your next career move, time is important, so don't waste any time by writing a long-winded plan. The quicker it is formulated, the sooner you can start the implementation process.

Keep it Simple Stupid 'KISS' your way to success.

Flexibility There is a fine line between being determined and being pig-headed. A successful business plan is a flexible living document and, therefore, should be reviewed on a regular basis. It is important to remember that your plan is not cast in stone. If your plan is not working, be prepared to seek alternative solutions and make the necessary changes, whether they are big or small. Keeping your plan flexible will also allow you to take advantage of any unexpected opportunities.

Having an adaptable and fluid plan is not the same as moving the goalposts every time you encounter an obstacle or get a new idea. The end result is still the same, to find suitable work, but the journey may change and take a different route based on any number of factors. Keep your eyes firmly on the finishing line and be disciplined in making changes when warranted.

Realism A successful career plan is built around achievable targets. Although these targets must stretch you and it is important to aim high, your plan must be based on reachable goals. Don't get carried away dreaming about a career that is just not feasible. A plan that is too high on aspiration is usually low on implementation.

When you are drafting your plan, you will be forced into making a lot of major decisions. Some will be very difficult and have a long-term effect on your career. Thinking about these decisions in advance will help you to maintain a clear focus on what you want to achieve.

"Everything gets written down, formally, so that you know at all times where you are, where you've been, where you're going and where you want to get. … because otherwise the problems get so complex you get lost in them and confused and forget what you know and what you don't know and have to give up."

Robert M. Pirsig

Written Writing down your business plan is a powerful exercise. It articulates exactly what your strategy is.

Your plan also helps you to decide if a chosen career path is really likely to fulfil your dreams and ambitions. Seeing it in writing allows you to get a feel for the type of work that you want to do.

It is also important that any amendments made to the original document should be updated in writing. Your business plan is a living document and requires reviewing at regular intervals. Revise your plan whenever there is a change in the market place. Although this constant updating may seem a little over the top, Tim Berry of www.entrepreneur.com writes:

> "While this might seem like chaos, it's actually the opposite; the constantly-updated business plan is what makes order out of chaos. It becomes a long-term planning process that sets up your strategy, objectives and the steps you need to take by constantly being aware of the results of these steps."

Signed off Your business plans for your career should be signed off by you and also dated. This displays your commitment to its implementation. It is your personal contract. Print it off and have it professionally bound.

What's in your personal business plan?

Business plans can vary in size and content and there are differing opinions on what should be contained in them. However, it is agreed that any type of written plan is better than no plan at all. The primary value in drafting a business plan is to have a written outline of your career strategy so that you can evaluate all aspects of its viability. It also serves as a document that you can give to others so that they can assess your chances of success.

Many entrepreneurs shy away from writing business plans, and this often leads to costly mistakes and lost time. Many argue that they have discussed their ideas and plans in detail and therefore they don't require a written plan. According to Terry Prone and Kieran Lyons, authors of *This Business of Writing*, you should not "kid yourself that talking about what you're writing is the same as writing. It isn't." You can talk all day about what you are going to do, but until you commit these tasks to paper they will inadvertently remain thoughts instead of actions. Prone and Lyons also tell us that:

> "Good professional writing always starts with [Rudyard] Kipling's 'six serving-men': What, Why, When, How, Where and Who, in no particular order."

"the constantly-updated business plan is what makes order out of chaos. It becomes a long-term planning process that sets up your strategy, objectives and the steps you need to take by constantly being aware of the results of these steps."

Tim Berry

Kipling's 'six serving-men': What, Why, When, How, Where and Who

This principle of good writing is a useful guide to establishing the content of your business plan. Study the following questions and begin to prepare your plan by carefully answering them.

What:
- Is the purpose of your business plan?
- Is your basic career strategy?
- Is your understanding of the employment market?
- Is your Unique Selling Point (USP)?

Why:
- Should anyone offer you work?
- Have you chosen this employment sector?
- Do you need to plan your career?
- Are you finding it hard to find a job?

When:
- Is the best time to find work?
- Will you start implementing your plan?
- Will you be headhunted?
- Should you review your skills?

How:
- Will you market yourself?
- Much time and money will you spend on your marketing strategy?
- Will you communicate your plan?
- Will you conduct your market research?

Where:
- Are the work opportunities?
- Are the threats to finding work?
- Are the weaknesses in your business plan?
- Are the gaps in your skills portfolio?

Who:
- Are your potential customers/employers?
- Will help you find suitable work?
- Are your competitors?
- Will prevent you from being successful?

Answering these questions allows you to capture a great deal of information that is specific to your career and is a powerful tool in writing your business plan. Gather as much data as possible, as this information will provide you with most of the content of your plan.

A good business plan should include the following headings:

- Executive Summary
- Background
- Services
- Market Analysis
- Marketing Strategy
- Financial Report

A good business plan should include the following headings:

- Executive Summary
- Background
- Services
- Market Analysis
- Marketing Strategy
- Financial Report

Executive Summary

The underlying purpose of the executive summary in your personal business plan is to introduce yourself, and your career strategy, to potential customers/employers. The executive summary communicates quickly what you have to offer; it makes it easy for the reader to see your capabilities and why they should meet you.

Keep it to a single page, the executive summary should outline a brief history of your work experience and the jobs market that you operate in. Always write it with your customer/employer in mind. Include your important successes, qualifications and relevant expertise. Outline the benefits you can bring to the reader. Capture the reader's attention and arouse their interest in you.

Background – Description of Yourself and Your Personal Goals

This part of the business plan highlights your personal profile and work experience. It is very similar to a well-written CV. You include background information and a description of the various industries or business sectors that you have worked in. Include important projects that you have been a part of, how they were successful and the role you played in their success. Outline any key positions that you held and current responsibilities that you hold. If you are changing business sectors, explain your reasoning and why you believe your decision to be correct.

Outline clearly how your previous work experiences will be applicable to any potential customer/employer. Link your profile to the specific market you intend to serve. Be thorough and factual. Be sure not to omit any key pieces of information about your experiences. Remember, decision-makers will be interested in reading your profile, so make it attractive and relevant to them. Be confident in your abilities and state clearly how you will enrich your customers/employers.

Explain in a few concise paragraphs your short-, medium- and long-term career goals. Again, link these goals to the employment sectors that you are interested in. It is also a good idea at this stage to outline who your potential primary customers/employers are likely to be and why they would be interested in what you have to offer. This helps any reader of your business plan to identify who your target audience is.

Finally, include in this part of your document your career development plans. It is useful for both existing and prospective customers/employers to see the potential growth and the business areas you wish to develop in. Later in the book we will discuss the importance of personal development and how to write your personal development plan.

Services – What You Have to Offer

This section of your business plan will outline precisely what services you have to offer to your existing and potential customers/employers. It may be the first time that you have written down the skills and experience you have developed over your working life to date. These skills are the assets of your business and what make you a success.

In this section you will also describe how you differ from or exceed everything else that is available on the employment market. This is where you have the edge – your Unique Selling Point (USP). Don't underestimate the value of USPs. Try to be a specialist, as this usually increases the amount that you can charge for your services. It also improves your employability if your specialism is in high demand but low in supply. However, do ensure that your area of expertise doesn't have a short lifespan.

It is important to spend time on this section of your plan and to get the content right, as this is the information that your customer/employer will focus their attention on. You need to instil confidence that what you offer is in fact what they need. You must capture the qualities that will relieve any pressure points being experienced by your customers/employers. Write about what you offer from the customer's/employer's perspective. Outline what *you* will do to help them, as your customer/employer is more interested in what you can do for them, rather than reading about your past glories. Approach it like a sales pitch, clearly outlining the benefits that you bring.

Every skill, and all of the knowledge and expertise that you offer must benefit your employer/customer. Show everyone why you are the best person to do the work that is on offer. Getting suitable work is highly competitive and you will need to be able to clearly articulate your profile and your USP. This will help you to demonstrate how you add value. The factors that support your claims should be outlined here. This is where you answer the question: "Tell me why I should offer you this position?"

Market Analysis

There are two parts to your market analysis. First, carry out research on your current customer/employer. Establish both their present and future needs so that you can position your services to meet these needs. Find out their criteria for career promotions or for getting involved in interesting projects.

The second part of your analysis deals with the external environment. If you are looking for opportunities outside of your current customer/employer, or if you find yourself unemployed, then you need a different approach. Start by defining your market; list the business sectors that you want to sell your services to. Research the various companies within your market. By carrying out a detailed analysis, you will become familiar with all aspects of your target market. It will indicate whether you are looking for work in a growth area, what level of income to expect and what are the competitive drivers. A comprehensive analysis is required to ensure the viability of your career strategy.

Now decide whether you want to work in a particular sector or use a particular skill. This will help you to focus your market research. Continue your analysis by determining the size of your target market, the trends and potential growth. Determine which customers/employers are hiring and whether they are in your geographical location or whether you are prepared to relocate.

Marketing Strategy

Once you have established your target market, you then work on your marketing strategy. A question that you must answer thoughtfully in this section of your personal business plan is: "how do I intend to inform the world that I am available for work offers?" The answer to this question sets the parameters for your marketing strategy. If you are unemployed then you can be very open in communication, you tell everyone. However, if you are currently working you will need to be more discreet in letting people know that you are open to offers. Business networking will greatly enhance your efforts in making the right people aware of your availability. (Networking is discussed further in **Chapter 6**.)

An effective marketing strategy will open doors for you. If marketing is not your strength then talk to someone with marketing experience and seek their help. A simple formula to help you promote yourself both internally and externally is the **AIDA principle**:

- **Awareness:** make people aware of what you have to offer in terms of your skills, knowledge

The AIDA principle:

- Awareness: make people aware of what you have to offer in terms of your skills, knowledge and expertise and that you are available.

- **Interest:** and expertise and that you are available.
generate interest in what you have to offer by outlining the benefits of your service from their perspective, how you solve a problem for them and how you add value to their business.
- **Desire:** make people fall in love with you and what you have to offer. Create urgency for your services. Show them what they are missing by not having you in their team.
- **Action:** make it easy for them to select you for their team.

- Interest: generate interest in what you have to offer by outlining the benefits of your service from their perspective, how you solve a problem for them and how you add value to their business.
- Desire: make people fall in love with you and what you have to offer. Create urgency for your services. Show them what they are missing by not having you in their team.
- Action: make it easy for them to select you for their team.

Financial Report

The final part of your business plan is the financial report. For any business to survive, its managers must be in tune with its financial position at all times. Running your career is no different. Writing a financial statement each month will provide you with an accurate picture of your ability to pay the bills and "remain in business". You don't have to be an accountant to draft simple financial statements. A basic income and expenditure account and balance sheet will suffice.

For any business to survive, its managers must be in tune with its financial position at all times. Running your career is no different.

It is best to begin by drafting a simple monthly income statement. Divide a sheet of paper into two columns. On one side write your source of income, how much you made and where it came from, and on the other side of the sheet write down all of your monthly outgoings. Total up each side to determine whether income exceeded expenditure. This will help you to understand the level of income that you need to run your personal business.

It is also a good idea to draw up a personal balance sheet, a snapshot of your personal financial strength at a particular moment in time. Similar to your income statement, you can compose a balance sheet by dividing a sheet of paper into two columns. On one side, list the source of funding for your career, including any loans or mortgages you have and the monies that you have put into your business. On the other side of the page list what you spend the funding on, such as your home, car and any other assets. The columns must balance.

Your business plan is an important document which you will use in many different situations. Some of the content will be used in your CV, other parts will be used to negotiate remuneration packages, bonuses or wage increases. Some parts of the plan will be used to evaluate your career options, whether to leave your current customer/employer or stay and continue to progress your career there. Overall, committing this document to writing together with the process of researching it will improve your focus on being employable.

Implementation Strategy

Implementation can be difficult. Most plans don't work out as expected. The reason for this is that plans are based on the future and, despite robust research, we cannot fully predict the future. In any case, unforeseen crises can occur that will derail the best thought-out plans. Indeed, even when we are aware of an impending crisis, we have a tendency to avoid dealing with the situation until the last possible moment.

However, regardless of these perennial problems, there are a few steps you should keep in mind when implementing your personal business plan.

A Step-by-Step Approach to Implementing your Personal Business Plan: The Virgin Land Approach™

The most brilliant business plans are worthless unless they are implemented.

The most brilliant business plans are worthless unless they are implemented. Your career plan is about getting results and improving your employability. To ensure that you are fully motivated to get your career up and running, answer these two questions:

- How determined are you to have a rewarding career?
- What would happen to you if your career failed?

When cultivating your career plan it is important to use my **Virgin Land Approach**™. This is a simple step-by-step method based on the old adage that the best crops are grown in a virgin plot which has a rich and fertile soil. The Virgin Land Approach™ gives you an opportunity to plan your career without any obstacles hindering your creativity and optimism. It isn't contaminated by any negative thoughts. It is a tool to challenge yourself when you write your **SMARTER** career objectives.

Most people, when thinking about how they can turn their goals into reality, start at the beginning and try to work their way towards their desired outcome. They spend a lot of time and energy trying to get started. Using this approach, many people give up when they encounter their first barrier. Their goal suddenly becomes more complicated and harder to achieve. It is too far away.

An easy way to improve your chances of success is to flip the traditional process around. Start the process by imagining that the goal is already achieved and work back towards the start. Document each stage of your journey, including any barriers or problems and how you overcame them.

> Start the process by imagining that the goal is already achieved and work back towards the start.

Experience from the training programmes on which I have used this method has shown me that it is beneficial for a number of reasons:

- It paints a realistic picture of what steps you need to take in order to achieve your goal.
- Small steps are easier to manage.
- It reduces the impact each barrier has on your overall goal.
- It establishes milestones.
- The journey back always seems quicker than the journey to a new destination.

To help you understand how the Virgin Land Approach™ could work for you, it's worth reviewing the sample vision statement used earlier:

Personal Vision Statement

I give my customer/employer continuous outstanding work by maintaining my drive to add value to them by exceeding their expectations at every opportunity. I have won Salesperson of the Year for the third time. I constantly strive to improve myself personally and professionally so that I can pursue a successful career that I enjoy and can overcome any challenges I face. I have just completed a Diploma in Managing People in which my final assignment was voted best in class. I review my skills quarterly to ensure that I remain a market leader in learning and development and the preferred choice of my customer/employer. I have been promoted to Sales Director for Ireland and the UK.

The Virgin Land Approach™ – Sowing the Seeds of Your Success

Step 1   Harvest Day

Step 2   tell your story

Step 3   complete a list of all the actions you took on the road to your Harvest Day

Step 4   complete a list of all the barriers and obstacles that you encountered on your journey

Step 5   carry out a comprehensive skills audit

Step 6   describe your feelings at Harvest Day

Step 1   Pick a time and date in the future to become your **Harvest Day**. This is the day when the goals that you set yourself have been achieved and your vision statement is a reality. For instance, you have been nominated for Salesperson of the Year. It is important that you now imagine yourself on this future day celebrating the announcement that you have won. Picture yourself enjoying the rich pickings of your harvest.

Step 2   Now **tell your story**. Write down in detail all the goals that you have achieved on your Harvest Day. Your goals can include things like mastering new skills, promotion, improving the work environment or simply being happy in your job. You decide what your goals are and how many you need to aim for. Use the **SMARTER** Way™ (see **Chapter 3**) when listing your goals.

Step 3   The next step is to **complete a list of all the actions you took on the road to your Harvest Day**. Take each goal and outline how you achieved it. Write down all the lessons that you learnt along the way. Each action that you list here are the steps that you need to take to successfully implement your plan. By starting with the end in mind you can focus on the outcome rather than barriers or potential problems. This also gives you a better understanding of what you need to do and the timeframe required.

    Beside this list, write down the details of all the people who helped you along the way. These are the key people who form your networking circle. Enlist as much help as possible, as it makes the journey easier.

Step 4   Complete a list of all the barriers and obstacles that you encountered on your journey. List only the real obstacles, not the perceived ones. Write down what proof you have that they are real obstacles. Note all the steps you took to overcome them and the people who helped you along the way. Again these are key people from your networking circle (see **Chapter 6**).

"We are continually faced by great opportunities brilliantly disguised as insoluble problems."
Lee Iacocca, former Chairman of Chrysler

Step 5   Carry out a comprehensive skills audit (see **Chapter 5**) to ensure you have all the necessary skills to achieve your key objectives. Identify any gaps and develop a strategy for dealing with them. This will form part of your personal development plan.

Step 6   Describe your feelings at Harvest Day. Bring all of your passion into this description. What rewards did you receive as a result of your achievements? Who was there to help you celebrate your success? What significant difference did the fruits of your labour bring to your life?

Once you have tried The Virgin Land Approach and successfully achieved your goals you should immediately focus on your next set of goals. Confidence grows with success.

"The first and most important step toward success is the feeling that we can succeed."
Nelson Boswell (British writer and journalist)

Leave all Negativity at the Door

Adopting the Virgin Land Approach™ to developing your career allows you to see where your career can go once you discard all the baggage that you currently carry around. It is this excess baggage that weighs heavily on your shoulders and slows you down. Your vision is often hindered by your personal clutter. Lack of career focus, lack of a plan, lack of energy and drive, are all indicators of personal clutter. Negative attitudes such as: "I don't have the right experience", "I never have any luck in finding jobs", are all draining you mentally. Get rid of any damaging clutter now. You should also minimise your interaction with negative people because they will prevent your progress. They start to drain you of energy and enthusiasm and will eventually derail you.

If you have lost your job or missed out on a well-earned promotion you need to let go of your anger and hurt. Feeling sorry for yourself won't win you any admirers and this baggage will make you look unattractive. You will be seen as weak and bitter, not the sort of person that a customer/employer would want to have on their team.

When it come to being employable it is vital that you eliminate all negativity. There is no room for it in your career. Customers/employers require people who are positive, possess the right attitude and can deliver what they promise. Surround yourself with positive people who will support you through the ups and downs of planning your career.

And Finally ...

A final thought on career planning for people who are still reluctant to plan. If you wish, you can gamble with your career and let your customers/employers dictate how your career should develop. They will decide on the future direction of your career, both in terms of the type of work you will do and the maximum income that you will receive. This is taking the easy route because you have passed on the responsibility to someone else. However, this approach can often lead you down a career path that doesn't interest you.

But as you have gambled and lost you will have no option but to follow the career path chosen for you by your customer/employer. Can you afford to gamble with your career?

Do's and Don'ts of the Planning Department: Your business plan to keep working

DO:

- ✓ **Be a Master**
- ✓ Plan for success. Seek out opportunities to develop your career.
- ✓ Create a vision statement that will encompass your desired career.
- ✓ Focus on the things that you can control.
- ✓ Write a thorough career plan.
- ✓ Be confident in your skills and expertise.
- ✓ Build a profile of the future work landscape.
- ✓ Design a storyboard that sells your vision statement.
- ✓ Outline a business plan for finding work.

DON'T:

- ☒ **Don't Be a Slave**
- ☒ Don't believe that a career is for other people.
- ☒ Don't leave career planning until you lose your job.
- ☒ Don't ignore updating your career plan until you are passed over for promotion.
- ☒ Don't gamble with your career.
- ☒ Don't let baggage weigh you down.
- ☒ Don't look for pity and feel sorry for yourself.
- ☒ Don't blame other people for your current situation.
- ☒ Don't spend more time planning holidays than planning your career.
- ☒ Don't allow the first obstacle to halt progress.

> **When was the last time you did this?**
>
> - Review your career options?
> - Analyse the job market that you are competing in?
> - Find out what your employer's/customer's future needs are?
> - Update your career plan?
> - Update/re-draft your CV?
> - Think about how to promote yourself?

Writing your career plan will greatly increase your chances of success in finding the right work for you. Therefore, before you read any further, take a break and start composing your career plan now.

PERSONAL THOUGHTS

What will I do differently tomorrow?

CHAPTER 3

QUALITY ASSURANCE: SET YOURSELF APART BY ADDING REAL VALUE TO YOUR CUSTOMER/EMPLOYER

Quick guide to this chapter

- Finding your winning edge
- What is outstanding customer/employer service?
- From appraisals to performance review
- Where do they go wrong?
- The main objectives of performance reviews
- The SMARTER Way Goal Setting System™
- Making your performance review work for you
- Keys to a winning performance review meeting

Finding your winning edge

Now that you have written your energising and inspiring personal business plan it is time to focus your attention on your customer/employer. Your employee mindset is gone and has been replaced by an entrepreneurial, customer/employer-focused mindset. The process of writing your business plan should have helped you gain a better insight into the challenges that lie ahead.

It is time to focus your attention on your customer/employer.

Competition for work between people who offer similar services, knowledge and expertise has intensified. The current

Competition for work between people who offer similar services, knowledge and expertise has intensified. The current jobs market is unforgiving and full of talented people like you.

"If a man is called a streetsweeper, he should sweep streets even as Michelangelo painted, or Beethoven composed music, or Shakespeare wrote poetry. He should sweep streets so well that all the hosts of Heaven and Earth will pause to say, here lived a great streetsweeper who did his job well."
Reverend Martin Luther King Jr

"I skate to where the puck is going to be, not to where it has been," was how one of the greatest ice hockey players of all time, Wayne Gretzky, explained his success.

"If you really want something, you can have it if you're willing to pay the price. And the price means you have to work better and harder than the next guy."
Vince Lombardi

jobs market is unforgiving and full of talented people like you. Often, the only difference between staff is the quality of their performance and their ability to consistently offer outstanding customer/employer service.

Holding a qualification or being able to complete specific tasks is no longer good enough to get you a job, or indeed to hold onto one. You need to be the best out there. Providing a consistently high level of performance, together with a service that exceeds the needs of your customer/employer is vital for your continued employability. Managing this relationship with your customer/employer requires a dynamic and proactive approach. You must be alert to their changing needs, be able to resolve issues before they become problems and also understand their expectations in order to exceed them. Top performers are always one step ahead of their competition and this gives them the edge.

The change in your mindset to that of an entrepreneur, together with your inspiring business plan, are your first steps towards creating a winning edge that will increase your chances of finding work and a sustainable income. The next challenge is to create your customer/employer strategy, which is linked to your high performance. The combination of quality service and high performance will give you a winning edge. You must always be one step ahead in the game, by thinking future as well as current needs.

Legendary American football coach Vince Lombardi's philosophy on success is simple:

"If you really want something, you can have it if you're willing to pay the price. And the price means you have to work better and harder than the next guy."

Lombardi's proviso for success may sound obvious, but how many of us are truly willing to pay that price? Are you willing to work harder and smarter than others so that you will remain employable? Have you become soft and complacent because of your "I'm just an employee" mindset? Do you pick up your wages each month without considering whether you have added real value to your customer/employer? Underperformance is like a bad recession – you can see it coming but fail to react quickly enough, and then the consequences hit you hard and can be very difficult to turn around.

Hard work is a prerequisite for success and with hard work comes discipline and mental strength. Discipline is about developing a plan of action that you believe in and that you execute in every detail. Vince Lombardi writes in his book *What It takes To Be #1* that:

> "Discipline helps you make the hard decisions. It helps you embrace and endure the pain associated with change. It helps you stay on track despite stress, pressure, and fear."

You need to have the discipline to ensure that every day you do something that adds value to your customer/employer and moves you ahead of the competition. Every day you need to work a little harder than everyone else. Every day you must make one extra phone call, you must complete one extra task. Discipline ensures that the small things add up to high performance and outstanding service. Discipline allows you to form winning habits.

Mental strength will allow you to keep sight of your goals, even in the most stressful and economically challenging times. It will keep you focused and calm while others struggle to cope with the current climate. Mental strength gives you confidence in your ability to be successful. In sport, in a tight game that is fast approaching its conclusion, it is the player or team that has the greatest mental strength that often wins. In golf there are thousands of players that can hit the ball as straight and as long as the top professional players, but only a handful can hold their nerve on the final day and win. This is why so many of the top professionals use sports psychologists to work on their mental strength. The workplace is no different; the top performers have developed a mental strength that allows them to deliver outstanding performance, even in the toughest conditions.

Hard work is a prerequisite for success and with hard work comes discipline and mental strength. Discipline is about developing a plan of action that you believe in and that you execute in every detail.

Mental strength will allow you to keep sight of your goals, even in the most stressful and economically challenging times. It will keep you focused and calm while others struggle to cope with the current climate.

What is outstanding customer/employer service?

Customer service is more than just keeping your customers happy. In a competitive marketplace, customers/employers are now demanding not just good but outstanding service. Outstanding customer service is about understanding your customers' needs and then adding real value that consistently exceeds their expectations.

In a competitive marketplace, customers/employers are now demanding not just good but outstanding service.

Every interaction with a customer impacts on the level of service received. One of the true pioneers of outstanding customer service was Walt Disney. His vision of customer service, that you should always "do what you do so well that they will want to see it again and bring their friends", is the bedrock of the Walt Disney Company's continued success today.

It costs on average five times more to attract a new customer than to keep an existing one.

Organisations spend a lot of time and money trying to improve their customer care programmes because it costs on average five times more to attract a new customer than to keep an existing one. In a market where price and quality of product are similar, it is usually the level of customer service that differentiates companies. The need to deliver outstanding customer service is equally applicable to your relationship with your employer. Your boss, current or potential, demands more of you than just doing your job. They are looking for talented people who are willing and able to "go the extra mile". They need people who are flexible and can meet new challenges. Customers/employers need innovative and "can do" people. Providing outstanding service will make you stand out from your competitors in the jobs market.

Providing outstanding service will make you stand out from your competitors in the jobs market.

How good is your customer/employer service?

Saying that you value your customers is easy, but truly valuing them can be a difficult task. During the boom years, how many companies actually invested time and money in improving customer service? Very few did – they didn't have to. Demand for services and goods outweighed supply. People didn't always have a choice of suppliers.

Transfer the principles of customer care into the business of running your career and you can start to appreciate the similarities. Over the last few years, you didn't need to look after your customer/employer. There was a shortage of labour. You could leave your job on a Friday and get another one on Monday. In times of economic boom, you can take your customer/employer for granted, in the same way companies can take their customers for granted. However, the jobs market has radically changed and you can longer afford to make assumptions about your relationship with your customer/employer.

Transfer the principles of customer care into the business of running your career

If you are dependent on just one customer, how well do you treat your most important source of income? Ask yourself some important questions:

If you are dependent on just one customer, how well do you treat your most important source of income?

- Are you always trying to please your customer/employer?
- Is your customer/employer king?
- Do you exceed your customer's/employer's needs?
- Do you make a conscious decision every day to give value for money to your most important customer?
- Are you confident that you will get top marks at your next performance review meeting?
- Will your customer/employer remember all of the outstanding service that you give them?

Learn to love your customer/employer before someone else does. There is nothing more heartbreaking than losing something you love. Believe it or not, other people are actively looking to take your place. They want your job and you need to show your customer/employer that they don't want it as much as you do.

Learn to love your customer/employer before someone else does. There is nothing more heartbreaking than losing something you love. Believe it or not, other people are actively looking to take your place. They want your job and you need to show your customer/employer that they don't want it as much as you do.

It is easy to assume that you are delivering a quality service because you haven't heard anything to the contrary. Some people come to work with their employee mindset and do their job. They miss a deadline here and there, make a few errors in reports and generally go about their work in a competent manner. One of Don Keough's (former CEO of Coca-Cola) rules on how to lose in business is to rely on "T-G-E: That's Good Enough" and "T-N-M-J: That's Not My Job!" Employees who think like this haven't received any

How to lose in business is to rely on "T-G-E: That's Good Enough" and "T-N-M-J: That's Not My Job!"

complaints, so believe that everything is fine. However, this way of thinking is simply not good enough. Such misguided assumptions are contributing factors as to why people miss out on job opportunities and promotions. They are simply failing to meet their customer's/employer's expectations. Also too many bosses fail to articulate their displeasure with someone's performance in a constructive way. They either give vent to their annoyance, which usually leads to conflict and loss of focus on the real issue – which is underperformance – or they simply say nothing which leaves a false impression of the actual performance levels of their staff. This disengagement between a boss and employee eventually leads to a breakdown in the relationship.

Performance Review Meetings

To improve the service that you provide to your customer/employer you must first fully understand their real requirements and then be in a position to receive honest feedback. Your **Performance Management System** is one of the most effective ways of establishing your customer's/employer's needs and expectations as well as receiving feedback on your performance. Pat Sheridan, in *Human Resource Management: A Guide for Employers*, writes that performance management "involves managers working proactively with employees, in a systematic way to raise individual and/or group performance under specific headings applicable to their individual jobs and/or team work, having regard to business needs and positive motivational principles". It is a collaborative process, and as a result provides an ideal platform to raise your performance level.

An integral part of any performance management system is the performance review meeting. In its simplest form, your **performance review meeting** is an excellent opportunity to find out how you can add real value to your customer/employer. A well-planned meeting is the perfect forum to gather all of their requirements in a prioritised format. It is also a vehicle to get some constructive and honest feedback on your performance level. You can estab-

To improve the service that you provide to your customer/employer you must first fully understand their real requirements and then be in a position to receive honest feedback.

Your performance review meeting is an excellent opportunity to find out how you can add real value to your customer/employer.

lish if your service has exceeded your customer's/employer's expectation. A good meeting should leave you in no doubt as to whether you are a top performer. Your review meeting should be treated as a "wants and needs" analysis session that will guide your high performance strategy.

Making your performance review meeting work for you

Today almost all the top performing companies in Ireland, the UK and the US have a performance management review system in place. The type of system varies from organisation to organisation. However, it is universally acknowledged that an effective performance management process will increase performance, motivate people to achieve their agreed goals and boost staff/manager relationships. When everyone puts the required effort into making sure the performance management system is effective and worthwhile, it becomes a win/win situation for all.

> When everyone puts the required effort into making sure the performance management system is effective and worthwhile, it becomes a win/win situation for all.

Review meetings play an important role in all performance management review systems and are now seen as part of good management practice. A review is carried out once a year, with some organisations having either half-yearly or quarterly updates. Your performance assessments are important as they are often used to determine your current standing within the organisation or if you are suitable for promotion.

> To make review meetings work for you it is essential that you eliminate negative thinking such as:
>
> - My manager doesn't take the review meetings seriously.
> - It is biased towards recent work and doesn't reflect my overall performance.
> - I can't change the past.
> - The goals are meaningless as they change regularly and are never updated to reflect those changes.
> - It's a form-filling exercise driven by human resources.
> - I haven't got the time to plan it properly.

Despite the role that review meetings play in most people's lives, research shows that most people don't utilise the opportunities that they offer to further their careers. In particular, they fall into the trap of viewing these meetings negatively.

Ask yourself a simple question before you proceed any further: "Do I get the best out of my performance review meetings?" If not, it is time to take action and make the review meeting work for you.

How to get the best out of the Review Meetings

For review meetings to work well, it requires your manager to possess good leadership skills and an ability to inspire you to achieve great results. It also requires an investment of time from both of you in the preparation and planning of the meeting. The performance review meeting usually sets the minimum standard that your company expects you to achieve. It does this through setting **SMART** goals. The ideal meeting should be a consultative one – you and your manager agree your goals and the level of support you require in achieving these goals. Most of the goals set are tasks related to your current job.

These agreed goals now set the minimum expectations' level of your customer/employer, and can provide you with a platform to demonstrate your star qualities by exceeding your customer's/employer's expectations. For instance, if one of your goals is the reduce costs by 15% then you should aim to achieve cost reductions of 18%. If you go on to exceed all of your goals in a similar fashion then you have improved your employability status because you have clearly demonstrated a capacity to deliver outstanding service.

While your company can control the minimum standard of productivity that they expect from staff, by contrast, you, as an individual, can control the maximum levels of productivity that you can deliver. It is your ability to turn this to your advantage that will help to determine the future growth of your career. Companies need to identify their star performers and ensure that they retain their services. The performance review meeting is the ideal forum in which to show your star qualities and receive credit for your outstanding performance.

These agreed goals now set the minimum expectations' level of your customer/employer, and can provide you with a platform to demonstrate your star qualities by exceeding your customer's/employer's expectations.

Companies need to identify their star performers. The performance review meeting is the ideal forum in which to show your star qualities.

Why do Performance Review Meetings go wrong?

The primary function of the performance review meeting is to tell you how you have performed during the year that has just passed. For many managers, it is a chance to tell you what you have done badly. It is also a mechanism for outlining your targets for next year. Research consistently shows that most employees believe that their performance review meetings or appraisals are really for the benefit of their employer. Frequently, it is viewed as a form-filling exercise designed by the Human Resources department and serving no real purpose. It is treated with a great deal of skepticism, particularly in today's recessionary times.

However, the performance review meeting will only be as effective and useful as the people using it. Its success will be determined by you and your manager. Many review meetings introduced into organisations with training, and to much fanfare, could now be running out of steam and may need to be revitalised. There are some simple reasons why your performance review meetings may not be as productive as when first implemented:

- Staff turnover and cutbacks in recent years could mean that many reviewers and reviewees may not have had the same training as those who were in the organisation when the performance review system was first introduced. In many cases, after the initial training to teach people how to conduct review meetings, most organisations do not provide follow-up training. Hence, many staff and managers learn how to conduct meetings, including their bias for or against the system, from their colleagues.

- Total apathy from senior management towards the performance review meetings may seem an odd reason that the performance review meeting itself is not effective, as these are the people who introduced the system in the first place. However, senior managers often feel that they are judged on results only and that they are too busy to spend the time reviewing their staff. Unfortunately, they also set the example for others, both good and bad and, as a result, if managers and staff witness this apathy then it is hard to motivate them to take these meetings seriously.

The performance review meeting will only be as effective and useful as the people using it.

- Lack of follow-up on points that were raised at the review meeting. No encouragement given to reviewees to help them achieve their agreed goals or targets. Many promises are made, but few are delivered. As a result the review system becomes a once-a-year form-filling exercise for the HR department.

- Today's environment is one of constant change. Systems and procedures that worked and achieved excellent results two or three years ago may no longer achieve similar results today. Organisations review their budgets, marketing strategy and the technology they employ on a regular basis, and make the necessary changes to ensure success. Your performance review meeting should be no different. It requires regular evaluation and improvement, yet organisations neglect this crucial device for motivating their most important asset: their staff.

Despite its numerous drawbacks, your performance review meeting can be used to your advantage. With careful planning and an investment in your time, a good meeting is the ideal opportunity to retrieve detailed feedback from your most important customer.

What are the objectives of your Performance Review Meeting?

The performance review meeting provides a process through which you can discuss openly with your manager how you have performed your job in general, your key tasks in detail and areas for improvement and development over the next review period. It is your opportunity to evaluate your performance and quality of service with your number one client. Never lose sight of the fact that your manager represents your customer/employer.

Your performance review also allows you to step back from your busy schedule and complete a **Relationship Stocktaking Analysis** (which will be discussed further in

Systems and procedures that worked and achieved excellent results two or three years ago may no longer achieve similar results today.

Your performance review meeting is the ideal opportunity to retrieve detailed feedback from your most important customer.

Chapter 6). You should make a list of the significant people you regularly interact with and describe your relationship with each. This list should include your manager, colleagues, people who report to you, and the people who support your career ambitions. You should compare this year's inventory of people with last year's to see if there are any notable differences. If there are differences, examine the reasons thoroughly. Pay particular attention to key power players and examine your relationship with them. These are the people who have the biggest influence on your career and, therefore, your employability. Are you in a stronger position this year than last year? Have you made significant progress in building these relationships? How have they helped your employability status? The answers to these questions will feed into your high performance strategic plan.

Your performance review meeting does not just measure your results against targets and objectives. It is an opportunity to carry out **a quality audit**, to assess your performance and to agree a mutually beneficial way forward. A well-thought out and balanced review meeting will ensure that you:

- have a clear understanding of your objectives and that your objectives are aligned to overall corporate objectives;
- are given feedback on your performance and are shown where you have added value to the organisation;
- have the necessary skills and knowledge to achieve your objectives;
- are supported by management and the organisation in your development;
- are part of the process of defining your key goals and development;
- leave the meeting with a clear understanding of your role and expectation within the organisation;
- know if you are on the "high flyer list" and how you are thought of by your manager and the organisation;
- are motivated to perform to your full potential over the next period.

> Pay particular attention to key power players and examine your relationship with them. These are the people who have the biggest influence on your career and, therefore, your employability.

- receive feedback on what help and support you need to perform even better.

It doesn't matter whether your manager believes in the performance review process or not, you should maximize the benefits of the review meeting itself through detailed planning and investing sufficient time in preparing thoroughly for it.

Successful people use the performance review meeting to enhance their career prospects and employability. It doesn't matter whether your manager believes in the performance review process or not, you should maximize the benefits of the review meeting itself through detailed planning and investing sufficient time in preparing thoroughly for it.

Keys to a winning Performance Review Meeting

Let me ask you a question that I have asked many people over the years: How much time do you spend preparing for your annual performance review meeting? Is it 30 minutes, an hour or whatever length of time it takes to fill out the review forms? If you view the review meeting in this way (and you wouldn't be alone), then you are missing out on the biggest opportunity that you will get to promote your career and receive feedback on your performance. Attending a review meeting without the necessary preparation is simply unprofessional. It sends out the wrong message. Would you visit your most important client without proper preparation?

Attending a review meeting without the necessary preparation is simply unprofessional. Would you visit your most important client without proper preparation?

Your performance review meeting should be seen as your showcase for the year. It is your opportunity to put on record all the reasons why you are the star of the organisation. You can share all your successes and your plans for the coming year with your manager, who represents your customer/employer. It is your opportunity to surprise and impress them. It is also your opportunity to carry out a customer/employer service audit and assess their needs. All of this requires careful preparation and investment of time.

Despite this, most of us turn up at our annual showcase unprepared, and consequently suffer severe stage fright. We stumble into the habitual pitfalls of bad and forgettable performance review meetings:

- Our presentation appears unprofessional
- We sell ourselves short
- We fail to engage our customer/employer in real conversation
- We suggest goals that are uninspiring and fail to add value
- We display our "employee mindset", and it looks totally unattractive
- Our performance at the meeting matches our performance during the year – basic, at times forgettable, and lacking impact.

To avoid this embarrassing scenario you must follow the **Three Ps** guide to perfect showcasing:

- Prepare,
- Plan, and
- Practise.

There is no shortcut to business success and employability. It is your career, you own it and, therefore, you have a responsibility for its success. Approach your performance review meeting as if it were an interview with a potential new customer/employer. Sell yourself all over again.

You can't over-prepare for Performance Review Meetings

How do you want to be remembered when you leave your performance review meeting? What positive impression did you make? Have you improved your employability status? Are you on the "rising star" list? The amount of preparation that you are willing to undertake will have a major impact on the success of the meeting and the lasting impression that you will make.

Begin the process of preparing for your next review meeting by carrying out some thorough **research**:

When was the last time you… ?

- Read last year's performance review?
- Reviewed your goals for this year?
- Completed your relationship stocktake?
- Established goals that would add value?
- Thoroughly prepared yourself for your review meeting?

The Three Ps guide to perfect showcasing:

- Prepare,
- Plan, and
- Practise.

How do you want to be remembered when you leave your performance review meeting?

- Look at the current format of your performance review meeting. Pay particular attention to the forms that require completing, the performance areas that are reviewed, and the structure of the meeting. Understand the scoring or rating system. Familiarise yourself with the process so that you have a clear insight into how your manager will conduct the meeting.
- Check out changes, if any, made during the year to the structure of the meeting, the goals that were agreed at the last meeting, or to the rating system.
- Review last year's report. Note any improvements that you may have made and ensure that you highlight them during the meeting.

Prepare your checklist under the following headings:

- What will the reviewer ask?
- How will you answer them?
- How will you deal with any difficult questions?

- Prepare your checklist under the following headings:
  - What will the reviewer ask?
  - How will you answer the questions asked?
  - How will you deal with any difficult questions?
- Appraise all your objectives and tasks for the period under review. If there are any tasks that are still outstanding articulate the reason why and your proposed strategy for dealing with it. Also, collect facts to support your accomplishments during the review period. Never assume that your manager will remember them.
- Think about setting SMARTER goals for the next period that will impress your manager as well as adding real value to your customer/employer. Invest sufficient time in this area, as it will lay the foundation for your performance next year.
- Review your achievement file (see below).

Plan your Review Meeting (or "Showcase")

Plan your review meeting with enthusiasm and in detail. Don't leave anything to chance. Determine which elements of your performance you want to convey. Also, review how you will answer key questions and the length of time that you will give to each of these answers. It is a good idea to check the wording of your answers to ensure that you will be clearly understood.

Here is a quick guide to your planning:

- Make a list of all the areas you want to discuss – your agenda.
- Budget your time to ensure each element gets equal airing and key points aren't omitted.
- Write down all your key points to act as prompts during the meeting. Bring brief notes with you.
- Be familiar with filling out the forms so precious time isn't wasted.
- Complete any pre-interview forms.
- Dress to impress, professionally and stylishly.

Practise

The more you practise, the easier it becomes. Carry out as many rehearsals as it takes. This is the most important meeting of the year. Rehearsing what you will say at the meeting will increase your confidence and professionalism. Your answers will appear natural and convincing. When practising you should:

This is the most important meeting of the year.

- Stand tall and project a positive image.
- Rehearse the meeting with a friend or colleague.
- Answer all difficult questions out loud.
- When you think you have it right, do it one more time.

Roll of honour

One of the main barriers to a successful performance review meeting is when it is based on your most recent performance rather than your performance over the full review period. This "**recency effect**" is due to the fact that neither your manager nor you can remember what you achieved perhaps six or seven months previously. Your focus is only on the most recent goals that you have achieved. However, this can distort how your overall level of performance is viewed.

Therefore, throughout the year it is vital that you constantly update your **"achievement file"** with your accomplishments. Many of us are reluctant to do this as it might be seen as big-headed or boastful, but when it comes to your achievements don't be shy about airing them. By detailing them over the year, you can quickly remember all the outstanding things you have accomplished before you go into your review meeting. It is also useful to update your CV with your current successes, and link each success to how it can add value to your customer/employer. It will paint a positive picture for them.

There is another advantage to keeping an achievement file. If you are ever feeling a little down or frustrated with your career progress, take some time out and read about your accomplishments. You will be astounded by what you have achieved to date. It will give you a boost and lift your spirits so that you can focus on delivering an outstanding performance.

Update your "achievement file" with your accomplishments.

If you are ever feeling a little down or frustrated with your career progress, take some time out and read about your accomplishments. You will be astounded by what you have achieved to date.

"Pleasure in the job puts perfection in the work."

Aristotle

The Most Common Pitfalls of Performance Review Meetings

- **Stress** – The interview becomes so stressful for you that you forget your rehearsed lines and consequently sell yourself short. Practise calming techniques.
- **Halo/Pitchfork effect** – The "halo effect" is when you display one great trait and your manager then believes that everything you do is great. Conversely, "the pitchfork effect" is when you display one bad trait and your manager then believes that your overall performance is poor. Relying on the halo effect can be a risky strategy as you are gambling on your manager seeing your one good trait. Don't leave this to chance.
- **Central tendency** – This is when your manager takes the easy option and rates everyone in the team as the same. Remember, don't settle for being equal. Stand out from the crowd and become the star. Make your manager recognise that your performance was superior to that of your colleagues.

Remember, don't settle for being equal. Stand out from the crowd and become the star.

- **Recency syndrome** – This is when your accomplishments are assessed on recent performance instead of your full performance. Review your achievements file and say what you have achieved over the full period. Ensure that you get credit for all of your work.
- **Personal biases** – Your manager likes Mary because she does a great job; or is it that she does a great job because your manager likes Mary? Keep the review factual and provide the evidence to support your performance.
- **Negative group think** – Avoid talking to dissatisfied and disillusioned colleagues before your review meeting – they can waste a lot of your energy. Break free from their negative mindset. It's your career that matters, not their approval.
- **Negative language** – Choose your words carefully so that you create and maintain a positive mindset during the review meeting. Do not bring negativity to the meeting.

Are you ready for your review meeting?

One of the biggest misconceptions about performance review meetings is the amount of preparation that you need to undertake. People believe that because the meeting is about their performance that they can just turn up and start talking about themselves. Unfortunately, a quarter way through the meeting they then realise that they can't remember key facts that would support the points that they wanted to make. Then the meeting moves to setting goals and they can't even suggest one goal for the next review period. You can never be over-prepared. If you haven't fully prepared for a review meeting before, then ask yourself the following questions:

One of the biggest misconceptions about performance review meetings is the amount of preparation that you need to undertake.

You can never be over-prepared.

> ## Performance Review Meeting Checklist
>
> - What, if any, aspects of your job description require amendment to accurately reflect the job you are now doing?
> - In which areas of your job do you think you have performed well?
> - How have you made a significant contribution to the work of the section/department?
> - Are there some areas of your job in which your performance could be improved? If so, what action do you feel you might take to bring about an improvement?
> - Are there some areas of your job, outside your control, that prevent you from achieving your desired performance?
> - What actions can be taken by you or by others that would bring about an improvement?
> - Which part of your job do you find easiest/hardest?
> - What are your development needs?
> - What tasks for the coming year do you think are important?
> - Do you produce the kind of results that your customer/employer requires from someone doing your job?

Motivation and Performance

Successful teams, whether in sport or the workplace, are made up of people who have the skills and knowledge to carry out the job, an understanding of their role and their team mates' roles, but, most importantly, are motivated. Motivation is integral to producing high performance. It also plays an essential role in being employable. Wanting to be employable is one thing, but being committed to ensuring that you are employable is something else. Real commitment requires self-motivation so that, whenever a barrier or obstacle is put in your way, you remain focused and driven to achieve your goal.

Wanting to be employable is one thing, but being committed to ensuring that you are employable is something else.

72

For years now people have been told to set SMART goals or tasks. SMART stands for **S**pecific **M**easurable **A**chievable **R**elevant and **T**ime bound. However, there is a **SMARTER way.** When you set goals that you are highly motivated to achieve, then you are well down the road to success. It's simple philosophy. There is no big mystery or secret formula to accomplishing great things. When you set a goal, you must get excited about completing that goal. You must bring energy, enjoyment, enthusiasm and effort to it. Then you must envision the reward, what you will get once you have successfully completed the goal. Important career goals need clarity and motivation so that nothing prevents you from achieving success.

Achieving important goals can be daunting. They can seem harder than they actually are. A simple but effective way to bring clarity and motivation to achieving your goals is to write them out using the SMARTER Way Goal Setting System™. When you set yourself a task, goal or job to do, there are two elements that will determine whether you will be successful:

- a clear understanding of the goal, and
- the motivation to achieve it.

When people decide to take responsibility for their employability they are often too vague when outlining their goals. They state the obvious, such as "I need to find a job" or "I love more challenging work". This is bland and lacks drive. You must get yourself excited about completing your goals, otherwise there is a distinct possibility that procrastination will take root. It is also important that you visualise your reward – what's in it for you. This system will ensure that you have a clear understanding of what you would like to achieve and the motivation to remain persistent in its successful completion.

The SMARTER Way Goal Setting System is defined as:

- **Specific**
- **Measurable**
- **Achievable**
- **Relevant**
- **Timeframe**
- **Exciting**
- **Reward**

There is a SMARTER way.
When you set a goal, you must get excited about completing that goal.

"It always seems impossible until it's done."

Nelson Mandela

There are two elements that will determine whether you will be successful:
- a clear understanding of the goal, and
- the motivation to achieve it.

The SMARTER Way Goal Setting System is defined as:

- Specific
- Measurable
- Achievable
- Relevant
- Timeframe
- Exciting
- Reward

Specific People often set career and personal goals that are simply too vague. "I want an exciting job," or "I want to improve my career prospects" are goals, but it is hard to determine whether you have achieved them or not. If there are no goalposts, how do you know if you have scored? However, if you rephrase your goal to "I want to improve my rating at my next review meeting" you now have a specific career goal. Setting a clear goal will mean that you cannot distort the result. A specific goal shows that you have either succeeded or that you need to try harder. It concentrates your mind on the result.

If there are no goalposts, how do you know if you have scored?

Measurable Achieving goals needs to have some form of measurement. As the old saying goes "what gets measured gets done". Incorporating a clear measurement in your written goal will make it easier to see if you have hit your intended target. The measure should be linked to a specific part of your goal. For example, "I want to improve my rating by moving up from a score of three to a score of four at my next review meeting" is a goal with a definite measurement. You can also break down the overall measurement into smaller, more achievable objectives. These smaller targets can become benchmarks or progress signs.

"What gets measured gets done."

Achievable Your goals should stretch you, but not break you. The success or failure of your goals can often be determined by the fact that the goal was unrealistic in the first place. Naïve goals set you up to fail, and run the risk of being abandoned before you even start. Equally, if your goal is too easy to achieve, the chances are it hasn't brought you any closer to being a master of your career.

Your goals should stretch you, but not break you.

Your goals should force you out of any comfort zone that you have fallen into. Try an idea that is challenging and will make a significant difference to your employability. Maintain a positive attitude towards achieving your goal. International leadership expert John Maxwell argues that:

"We cannot control life's difficult moments but we can choose to make life less difficult. We cannot control the negative atmosphere of the world, but we can control the atmosphere of our minds. Too often we try to choose and control things we cannot. Too seldom we choose to control what we can – our attitude."

A positive attitude builds your entrepreneurial mindset and moves you further away from just thinking like an employee. It gives you the determination and drive to succeed.

A positive attitude builds your entrepreneurial mindset and moves you further away from just thinking like an employee. It gives you the determination and drive to succeed.

Relevant Avoid setting goals that aren't relevant to improving your level of performance. Relevant goals will ensure that all of your effort is devoted to achieving your vision for yourself (your business). The relevance of your goal should be aligned to your motivation to improve. This will ensure that you work SMARTER rather than harder.

Timeframe There is nothing like an impending deadline to concentrate the mind. We think and talk about how we wish we had more time to spend doing what we would like to do rather than the things that are imposed on us. We also bemoan the fact that there aren't enough hours in the day to complete all of our tasks. This is often the excuse we use for not planning our careers!

We bemoan the fact that there aren't enough hours in the day to complete all of our tasks. This is often the excuse we use for not planning our careers!

Most people never take action to implement career goals that would improve their employability because they don't set deadlines. As a result there is never a sense of urgency, and procrastination takes root. Unless something drastic happens, such as redundancy, they fail to set career goals. Therefore, set realistic but challenging timeframes. Make them too short and you will become disillusioned because you are not progressing as quickly as you had hoped. By contrast, if the timeframe is too long you will waste a lot of time waiting for things to happen.

Decide on your starting time (within the next 24 hours) and then calculate your finish date. Estimate how long each task will take to complete allowing for normal delays. Include some milestones that will help you to track your progress and ensure that you are on schedule to complete your goal on time.

Exciting Make sure your goals are full of the right **Es**: exciting, enthusiasm, energy, entrepreneurship and enjoyment. Write out why your goals are exciting. Bring passion to your desire to achieve your goals. Energise those around you with your enthusiasm for success. Ensure that the key supporters of your career plans are also excited about your wish to improve your employability.

Every day you should be excited about moving closer to your vision for yourself...
enjoy the journey

Every day you should be excited about moving closer to your vision for yourself (your business). Talk enthusiastically about your goal; focus on why you want to achieve this goal of mastering your career. Make sure your energy levels are high as this will drive you forward. Finally, enjoy the journey as this is your goal, your life, your success.

Reward What will you achieve as a result of completing your goals? List the many benefits that achieving your goals will bring you as this list will improve your motivation to be successful. Always keep your eye on the prize. You should also outline the benefits that your customer/employer will enjoy as you may need their support or approval en route.

Add incentives to your journey so that you can maintain your drive throughout your progress to peak performance. Achieving challenging goals isn't easy – it requires dedication, perseverance and a real desire to improve. If your reward is big enough you will ensure that there are no barriers that will prevent you from being successful. Visualise the end result. Write down how you will feel when you achieve your goals.

The lifeblood of your journey

Visualising and writing down your goals will become the lifeblood of your journey to sustained employability.

Visualising and writing down your goals will become the lifeblood of your journey to sustained employability. While the **SMART** part of your goals gives you a clear understanding of what you have to do and the timeframe within which you will achieve your goal, the final "**ER**" part is the motivational drive behind your goals. This is the difference between talking about what you should do and actually committing yourself to action and doing it.

Achieving outstanding results is based on your ability to be excited and enthusiastic about your goals and to clearly understand what your rewards are. Why you need to improve your performance levels, and what's in it for you when you do, are the two key questions that you must answer honestly. These answers will help you to get back on track if your plan starts to unravel or you become despondent or lose interest. Champions have a clear vision of their goal. How they achieve the goal might change but their goal remains fixed in the mind; this winning mindset never waivers.

Using the SMARTER Way Goal Setting System will transform your career goals into desirable and attainable tasks. This system will convert wishing into wanting, and then into achieving. It will help you move from the limitations of an employee mindset into a liberating entrepreneurial way of thinking.

Writing down your goals will increase your chances of success

A study on goal setting sponsored by the Ford Foundation found that only 10% of Americans had clearly defined goals, and 7 out of 10 of these achieved their goals only half the time; 3% of people, however, achieved their goals 89% of the time. The reason for the high success rate among this small group was that **they simply wrote down their goals**.

The SMARTER Way Goal Setting System in action

To help you understand how the **SMARTER Way Goal Setting System** method could work for you, it's worth reviewing a typical goal or task.

Career goal: "I will deliver a sales presentation to our local trade community, which will promote my company's new product range. This presentation will be delivered at the

Why you need to improve your performance levels, and what's in it for you when you do, are the two key questions that you must answer honestly. These answers will help you to get back on track if your plan starts to unravel or you become despondent or lose interest.

Using the SMARTER Way Goal Setting System will:

- Get you started within the next 24 hours
- Provide you with a measurement for success
- Give you a clear understanding as to why you need to improve
- Help you get what you really want from your career
- Keep you motivated and focused
- Enhance your entrepreneurial mindset
- Enable you to clearly state your rewards
- Build persistence which will help you overcome the barriers
- Give you the edge
- Focus you on achieving peak performance

The reason for the high success rate among this small group was that they simply wrote down their goals.

next business networking meeting which will be held in four weeks' time."

Specific	to deliver a sales presentation to promote new product range
Measurable	positive feedback from audience; increase in sales figures for following month
Achievable	my colleagues have carried out similar sales presentations
Relevant	good for company profile; increase sales figures
Timeframe	within four weeks
Exciting	to improve presentation skills
	to push myself out of my comfort zone as I haven't done one before
	to further build my skills set
Reward	sense of achievement
	generate additional income for company
	raise my personal profile
	develop my personal brand

Personal goal: "I will learn to speak Spanish to Level 1 by the end of the college term."

Specific	I will learn to speak Spanish
Measurable	pass the oral exam at Level 1
Achievable	I learned to speak Italian two years ago
Relevant	I visit Spain regularly on holidays and business
Timeframe	by the end of the college term
Exciting	to improve my language skills
	to push myself
	to communicate with my Spanish friends and work colleagues in our Spanish office
Reward	sense of achievement
	make better use of my trips to Spain
	have another language as an asset
	expand career options in our Spanish office
	develop my personal brand

If you are looking for a new job

Your customer/employer, both current and potential, are all looking for the same thing – talented people who can deliver a high performance, consistently. They need people with the right attitude, desire and a capacity for change. They need outstanding service.

If you are currently looking for a job it is important to tailor your customer/employer strategy to finding work. A standard CV gives the impression that you are a standard performer. It lacks creativity, a desire to make an impact. It shows that you have settled for using the same strategy for finding a job as everyone else.

Develop your CV to highlight how you can offer real added value to your potential customer/employer. Your CV should demonstrate clearly what you can do for your new customer/employer. Tailor or customise every CV to the job on offer. Don't use your CV to list all of your achievements unless they are relevant to the person who is reading it. Work out their needs and show how you can exceed these needs.

Present your CV as if it were a promotional brochure. Keep it attractive and concise. Highlight features such as experience and qualifications and present them as benefits for the potential customer/employer. On application, you will only get 20 seconds to hold their interest, so grab their attention with an attractive CV.

> Your customer/employer, both current and potential, are all looking for the same thing – talented people who can deliver a high performance, consistently.

> A standard CV gives the impression that you are a standard performer.

> Tailor or customise every CV to the job on offer.

> On application, you will only get 20 seconds to hold their interest, so grab their attention with an attractive CV.

Do's and don'ts of your quality assurance department
Set yourself apart by adding real value to your customer/employer

DO:
- ✓ **Be a master**
- ✓ Demonstrate your winning edge by consistently giving outstanding customer/employer service.
- ✓ Get the best out of your performance management system.

✓ Include at least one SMARTER goal that will add value to your career.

✓ Take responsibility for any training that was agreed with your manager to ensure it takes place.

✓ Align your career goals to the company's business plan.

✓ Collect evidence of how you have performed above the agreed standard during the last review period.

✓ Show your willingness to take on additional key responsibilities that will add value to your career.

✓ Use the review sessions to build your brand awareness. Show your professionalism throughout the process. Have the discipline and the mental strength to deliver outstanding performance. Use your performance review meeting as a wants and needs analysis session to gather all of your customer's/employer's requirements.

✓ Set your goals using the SMARTER Way Goal Setting System.

DON'T:

☒ **Don't be a slave**

☒ Don't become soft and lazy because of your employee mindset.

☒ Don't see your performance review as for managers only.

☒ Don't use excuses for your failure to prepare properly.

☒ Don't settle for a good performance.

☒ Don't fail to find out what the overall business goals are.

☒ Don't write a standard CV.

Before you read any further, take a break and write down how you are going to add value to your customer/ employer.

PERSONAL THOUGHTS

What will I do differently tomorrow?

CHAPTER 4
MARKETING:
PROTECT YOUR PERSONAL BRAND

Quick guide to this chapter

- What is personal branding?
- Carry out a detailed self-analysis
- Develop your personal brand
- Create and practise your personal commercial
- Understand your unique value proposition (UVP)
- The "dating game"
- Cold calling for an interview

The secret to your success is not to keep it a secret

If there is nothing special about you or your work, you are unlikely to get noticed. If you are not adding real value to your customer/employer, your importance is devalued. When it comes to doing the accounts at the end of the financial year you will be itemized, along with the office furniture, computers and any other assets required to run the business. You are merely a number on a spreadsheet. Consequently, there is a danger you will become as disposable as the furniture you are sitting on. In today's dynamic and ultra-competitive jobs

There is a danger you will become as disposable as the furniture you are sitting on. In today's dynamic and ultra-competitive jobs market if you don't get noticed, it's likely you will receive your notice.

market if you don't get noticed, it's likely you will receive your notice.

One way to make an impact in a positive way is to turn yourself into a marketable brand. A strong personal brand will promote you from the chorus line into star billing. By having your name in lights, mounting a clever advertisement campaign and consistently delivering on your promises, you can become a valuable employee within your organisation, someone your boss will choose when the attractive work is on offer. Creating a memorable brand that people want to be associated with can make all the difference when it comes to who stays and who goes.

What is branding?

In its simplest terms a brand is a promise to deliver a service or product to a certain standard. Given the right image, a brand can send a powerful and positive message to the consumer. Great brands are worn like medals of distinction and honour: the Apple logo on an iPod, the prancing horse logo on a Ferrari, and so on.

Effective branding has become critical to the success of many businesses in an increasingly competitive market. Businesses whose aim is to grow and prosper need a strong and effective brand. This requires careful thought, planning and investment.

Companies over the years have used intelligent branding strategies to influence the purchaser. They have fostered customer loyalty through marketing campaigns, which send the message that it is good to be associated with their brand. They often appeal to our need for self-esteem. Certain brands are linked to film, music or sports stars. Their sex appeal invites you to purchase the products that are associated with them, and promise the feel-good factor when you do buy their products.

A strong and desirable brand allows a company to charge a premium price for its goods or services, as is the case with expensive designer clothing. It is no surprise then that companies are very protective of their branding.

Transfer the principles of great branding into the business of running your career and you will start to appreciate the similarities.

Does your personal brand justify your ability, skills and your image?

Whether you are an individual, a large multinational or a clothes designer the same principles for branding apply. You need to make yourself stand out from the crowd. Your current place of employment is full of products, services and people that work effectively and efficiently. Therefore, it is vital that you understand what makes you different and appealing. What is it about you that inspires and excites everyone around you?

Your personal brand is the image you portray to your customer/employer every day. It is your reputation. Your personal brand is built up through every interaction that takes place between you and your customer/employer. Their perception of you can be positive or negative, depending on their experience of working with you. According to the research company Gartner:

> "an experience is defined as the sum total of conscious events. As such, a supplier cannot avoid creating an experience every time it interacts with a customer."

A customer's/employer's experience will be heavily influenced by the expectation levels promised by your brand. Personal branding allows you to take control of what you promise to deliver. It tells people what they are going to get when they deal with you in any capacity. Develop a strong personal brand and it will help control your destiny.

However, the business world in which you currently work can be very unforgiving of brands whose promises don't match their delivery. Don't make the mistake of creating a brand that over-promises and under-delivers. Ensure that your message is authentic, as most people know the difference between what is real and what is not. Personal branding is not about brash statements with no substance behind

Whether you are an individual, a large multinational or a clothes designer the same principles for branding apply. You need to make yourself stand out from the crowd.

Your personal brand is the image you portray to your customer/employer every day. It is your reputation.

Aim a little lower but at the same time excite your customer/employer with the service that you offer and then surprise them by over-delivering.

Your personal brand will promote awareness of you and demonstrate why customers/employers must purchase your services on a regular basis. In fact they wouldn't risk being without you.

It is important that the right people know what you can do for them.

"Successful personal brands need to be authentic, have a good reputation, and be discovered by the right people."

Dan Schawbel

them. Fake brands may survive in the short-term, but in the long-run they are found out and dumped. Aim a little lower but at the same time excite your customer/employer with the service that you offer and then surprise them by over-delivering. When you exceed their expectations and they are delighted with your performance ask them for a testimonial. Over time these testimonials will form part of a work portfolio, which you can show to future customers/employers.

Developing a valuable and desirable personal brand is your way of sending positive messages to your current and future customers/employers. As an entrepreneur, you can join other business leaders and deliver an outstanding customer/employer experience. Nobody can prevent you from deciding that you are prepared to work hard at being exceptional. Building a powerful story is your opportunity to differentiate and create a source of competitive advantage. Your personal brand will promote awareness of you and demonstrate why customers/employers must purchase your services on a regular basis. In fact they wouldn't risk being without you.

Successful communication of your personal brand will elevate your standing with your existing and potential customers/employers. These are the people that you need to impress. Keeping your message under wraps is not an option if you want the type of work that excites you. It is important that the right people know what you can do for them.

Develop your brand

Successful branding sets you apart from your competitors.

The challenge is to build a successful personal brand that encompasses your personal values, attributes and vision. It must also be based on your customer's/employer's needs and you must link their values to your brand promise. You must be sure that your brand matters to them and that it provides a competitive differentiation. Successful branding is about delivering a clear and desirable message, which spells out why you add value to your customer/employer. It sets you apart from your competitors.

Consider the following **steps as you develop your personal brand:**

Step 1   Establish all of your customer's/employer's **moments of truth.** Jan Carlzon, the famed CEO of Scandinavian SAS Airlines and author of *Moments of Truth* described them as those moments when a customer interacts with your brand. It is in these critical moments that an impression about your brand is formed – for good or ill.

Review your moments of truth to determine whether your customer/employer has been left with a good or bad impression of their interaction with you. Discover whether they were disappointed or delighted with the service that you provided. Review this analysis from your customer's/employer's viewpoint. Mapping these critical points will allow you to put forward improvements that will enhance their experience and reduce any potential negative effects.

> It is in these critical moments that an impression about your brand is formed – for good or ill.

Step 2   Identify your main strengths and your sought-after assets. Think of this exercise as writing your own reference. What would you like people to say about you? Enlist your friends and work colleagues to help you draw up this list. They may add some qualities that you may feel are unimportant, but list them anyway. This is not the time to be reserved or shy about exposing your true value. Keep this list as long and broad as possible. Call your list of strengths and assets your "**desirable factors**".

Step 3   Answer the question: "What qualities in your desirable factors' list are essential to achieving your customers'/employer's objectives?" This is an important stage in tailoring your brand to appeal to the right people or "market". A carefully thought-out answer to this question will develop your **unique value proposition (UVP)**. This will help you to position yourself positively in the mind of your customer/employer. By choosing a few powerful words from your desirable factors'

> "What qualities in your desirable factors' list are essential to achieving your customers'/employer's objectives?"

list you will create a perception of value and differentiation, which will hook the right people more often.

As a professional you are passionate about exceeding expectations. Knowing what your customer's/employer's needs and wants are, and then aligning your desirable factors to them, is essential to building a powerful personal brand. It positions you for success.

Step 4   Write your brand statement. This will grab attention and will describe how you are a benefit to your customer/employer. It outlines the summary position of your brand by highlighting your main attributes. Keep it short, while answering these key questions:

- What does your personal brand offer?
- Who is your target market?
- What proof exists to support your brand benefits?
- What image does the brand need to reflect?
- What role will your brand play in achieving your customer's/employer's objectives?

Tell your brand story and excite your customer/employer. Ensure that you use words that convey energy and enthusiasm. Your brand statement is the proof required to support the benefits you offer.

How to use your Personal Brand to make Progress in your Current Job

- List the words that illustrate your best qualities. For example, creative, prolific, strong work ethic, make-it-happen attitude, etc. You can ask a friend or colleague to help you with this list. Read your previous performance review reports to see which qualities your boss has used to describe you and add them to your list. Now update your "**desirable factor**" file with any additional qualities from this list.

- Identify the personal qualities that are essential to carrying out your current job to the highest standards. Ask your boss for a detailed person specification for your current job or a job on offer. Ask them what the characteristics of their ideal worker are. Call this list of qualities the "The In-Crowd". Find out the qualities that your boss views as essential when deciding who is top of the "The In-Crowd" list. Don't forget your boss is your most important customer when it comes to career development.

- Compare your desirable factor file with the "The In-Crowd" list. Establish any reasons why you can't be top of "The In Crowd" list and start to bridge any gaps between the lists. You can also decide if you want to bridge any gaps or move on to another job.

- Use your personal brand to help you land future positions within your company by analysing the person specification for the job that you would like to fill within the next two years. Identify the competencies that best suit this job. Review your desirable factor file and establish any gaps in your file.

What does your personal brand say about you?

Your personal brand is your promise to deliver a service to a certain standard to your customer/employer, work colleagues, family and friends. It often determines how others perceive you. Your brand should remain consistent and focused. Effective branding will bring you to the attention of eager "buyers" and over time you will create a brand loyalty. Eventually, they will seek you out and you will become part of the headhunted community.

Your brand values are the powerful and positive things that your customer/employer feels when they think about you. This emotional experience builds a strong bond. You can send out many messages about yourself through your carefully nurtured brand. These will depend on the needs of your customer/employer at the time, and could include qualities such as:

- ✓ a strong personal work ethic
- ✓ reliability
- ✓ innovation and the desire to continually improve
- ✓ desire to succeed and be constantly challenged
- ✓ positive, "can-do" mindset

Once you have developed your brand and you are satisfied with the results, it is then time to reveal your assets. The unveiling of the new you could be the springboard you need to launch the next phase of your career. It is time to position yourself for success.

Unlock the benefits of personal branding

The value of your personal branding can be measured against the goals you set yourself. Your brand becomes more marketable and its value increases as these targets are achieved. Quality people are hard to find and, as a result, most companies are prepared to pay a premium for a superior brand. You can unlock the true value of your brand by charging a

---

Your personal brand is your promise to deliver a service to a certain standard to your customer/employer, work colleagues, family and friends. It often determines how others perceive you.

You can send out many messages about yourself through your carefully nurtured brand.

premium for your services when your customer/employer recognises that it needs you.

Other benefits include the feel-good factor, being held in high esteem and being a market leader. Remember, you want to be the number one brand in your organisation. This means that everything you say, think and do is of the highest standard as you are now the barometer for success. Instead of following standards, take a risk and set them. Become exceptional.

Remember, you want to be the number one brand in your organisation.

Your Personal Commercial

Creating a successful personal brand is only part of the picture. You also need to sell that winning formula. To maximise the opportunities that your brand unlocks, you need your target market to know about you, desire you and then take the necessary actions to promote you or, if you are in the job market, to hire you.

Your message must be heard. Great products have winning commercials, which serve two purposes:

Your message must be heard.

- to make people aware of something new, or
- to remind people of how much they need the product.

Great careers should also have winning commercials. Producing your own personal commercial will be fun and hugely rewarding. You have a compelling story to tell, so tell it.

A personal commercial for your career is simply a **30-second memorised description of what you have to offer** your customer/employer and any potential customers/employers. It is used to engage people, to arouse interest in what you have to offer and how you can add value to them. It is concise, informative and memorable. A great commercial will get the dialogue flowing between you and your customer/employer.

A personal commercial for your career is simply a 30-second memorised description of what you have to offer your customer/employer and any potential customers/employers.

There are many situations where you can use your personal commercial to sell your brand: when you are visiting a client, out networking with important business contacts; or just mingling at a party. After exhausting the usual

After exhausting the usual meaningless conversational icebreakers there is a pause. Someone usually then asks you what you do for a living. During the next few minutes you could either give a bland general answer or you could sell yourself and your career with a winning commercial. You could excite people, grab their attention and sell them the benefits of your services.

Successful companies sell themselves with a winning and memorable commercial, and so should you.

meaningless conversational icebreakers there is a pause. Someone usually then asks you what you do for a living. During the next few minutes you could either give a bland general answer or you could sell yourself and your career with a winning commercial. You could excite people, grab their attention and sell them the benefits of your services.

However, most of us blurt out unrehearsed, unassuming answers. "I work for…" or "I'm in the financial services sector", or whatever business sector they happen to work in, are common replies to this important question. These are bland, safe, going nowhere answers, just like the image they portray of a career. You need to come alive, break out of your comfort zone and step into the spotlight. Your career is important, exciting and going places. Successful companies sell themselves with a winning and memorable commercial, and so should you. Every business interaction is an opportunity to sell yourself and make an impressive impact.

It isn't easy, but is it worth it?

Five Steps to your "Personal Commercial"

1. Target Audience	A person who could influence your career
2. Your Product	Creative description of what you do
3. Their Need	Probing questions that lead to a need
4. You Provide	Description of benefits – reasons why you can help
5. You Excel At	Unique value proposition – link back to need

When writing a personal commercial you need to remain focused on the fact that this is a chance to sell yourself and gain a positive response from someone who could influence your career, whether it's internally or an external business client. You need to target your message carefully. This may require you to tailor it to suit different audiences.

Scripting your commercial is not easy and that is why most people opt for the safe, bland and general answer. But if you want to be steps ahead of your business rivals you should write a personal commercial now by following these simple guidelines.

Step 1 – Target Audience Your commercial should have a specific target market and it should be designed with this in mind. Your target market is the people that can influence your career and ensure your employability. Earlier in this book, you carried out some market research, so your target market should be identified at this stage. It contains your current customer/employer and all of your potential customers/employers.

The opening segment of your personal commercial will simply introduce you and where you work. Sell yourself confidently. Smile as you deliver it.

Seek to develop a meaningful relationship with your customer/employer. Use positive language – be enthusiastic.

It is important to note that this opening sentence can switch someone on or off. Therefore, keep it simple and engaging. Briefly say what you do and what is unique about your company and then the company name. This can create interest and credibility.

> "Hi I'm Sean and I'm the senior learning consultant with Europe's largest independent software company, ABC International."

However, if for instance you are networking within your organisation and you are introduced to a senior manager, your 30-second commercial could be tailored as follows:

> "Hi, I'm Sean and I work in our Training and Development Academy as a senior consultant with responsibilities for improving the performance of all of our staff."

Your target market is the people that can influence your career and ensure your employability.

"A man without a smiling face must not open a shop."
Old Chinese Proverb

"Nothing is so contagious as enthusiasm."
Samuel Taylor Coleridge

93

Make your job sound attractive and of high value, as this is the product you are selling. Remember all the work you did on your personal brand – now is the time to use it.

Step 2 – Your Product This is where you creatively tell your customer/employer what you do. Make your job sound attractive and of high value, as this is the product you are selling. Remember all the work you did on your personal brand – now is the time to use it.

"Hi, I'm Sean and I train our new staff" is not a compelling opening statement. It doesn't provoke an interest or response. You need to understand your product (your job) and how best to describe it. Use words that send a positive message. You are important and the person you are talking to must realise this immediately. Try something like the following:

> "Hi, I'm Sean and I work in our Training and Development Academy as a senior consultant with responsibilities for improving the performance of all of our staff. I specialise in rapidly up-skilling new and existing employees to ABC's high performance standards. This ensures that departments like yours do not suffer loss of productivity or a reduction in customer service during staff changes."

This commercial immediately sends the message – I'm important, I have an important job and I play an important role in making your job easier. I understand our company's culture and I play a pivotal role in maintaining our high standards of customer care.

Now that you have created an interest with your new contact, let's move in for a response. You need to find out if they are interested and how they can help with your career. After all, networking is another form of flirting.

Step 3 – Their Need Let's identify some probing questions that you can use to elicit a response. A little probing will establish a need from your potential customer/employer and you want to identify their "pain" or "problem" so that you can ease it with your product. So think carefully before choosing your questions as you may only get one chance. Your questioning should start with an open question, as this will entice your customer/employer to talk, followed by probing questions to elicit valuable information.

Questions to Establish a Need

Effective questions will unearth valuable information from a customer/employer in order to establish a "need". Try using some of the following question formats:

- ✓ What do you look for ... (e.g. when a staff member joins your team from a training perspective) (link to what you offer)?
- ✓ What have you found ... (to be your biggest challenge this year)?
- ✓ What do you need your team to be doing more of?
- ✓ How has your team dealt with the changes this year?
- ✓ Why is that a deciding factor ... ?
- ✓ Who in your opinion should I contact to get a decision about ...?

Effective questions will unearth valuable information from a customer/employer in order to establish a "need".

Let's look at how this personal commercial is shaping up:

"Hi, I'm Sean and I work in our Training and Development Academy as a senior consultant with responsibilities for improving the performance of all staff. I specialise in rapidly up-skilling new and existing employees to ABC's high performance standards. This ensures that departments like yours do not suffer loss of productivity or a reduction in customer service during staff changes. ..."

Now is a good time to ask a strong opening question such as:

"What do you look for, from a training perspective, when a staff member joins your team?"

You should always have a couple of probing questions at the ready. Once you have asked the opening question listen carefully to the reply. Carolyn Marland, managing director of the Guardian Group, sums up the importance of effective listening: "If you don't listen, you don't sell anything."

"If you don't listen, you don't sell anything."

Carolyn Marland

95

It is important to clarify the need if necessary, as this will galvanise the interest from your prospect. At all time you must be aware of the fact that you are building a relationship with this person:

> "So am I right in saying you place a huge importance on new staff understanding the principles of good customer care?"

Step 4 – You provide Once you have established and clarified the need, it is time to sell your customer/employer the benefits of what you provide. This is the "I need that" part of the commercial. It is, therefore, critical that you fully understand your product, including why and how you can help your customer/employer.

Most people sell the features of their product/service (I do this and I do that), but your potential customer/employer is not interested in what you *do*. Remember: you opened your commercial by creating an interest and then you got a response by carefully choosing your questions. Your potential customer/employer is only interested in how you can benefit them. You don't sell features; you sell **benefits**. You sell how you make their life easier by getting rid of their "pain" or "problem", through answering a need.

You can turn the features of what you offer in terms of skills, knowledge and expertise (your product) into benefits to your customer/employer with the help of a little phrase:

> "**... which means that ...**"

The best way to make this phase work for you is to memorise the key features of your product. Then listen carefully for the needs that your customer/employer outlined in response to your probing questions. Now explain the key features of your product that are relevant to these needs and then with the help of the phrase "which means that" go on to explain how this feature will benefit them.

Let's look at how this works. In the sample commercial discussed above, the need outlined by the customer/ employer is that they want their staff to have "a full under-

Your potential customer/employer is only interested in how you can benefit them. You don't sell features; you sell benefits. You sell how you make their life easier by getting rid of their "pain" or "problem", through answering a need.

"which means that"

standing of our customer service culture". The key feature of the training programme is "during our induction and retraining programme I show our corporate video on *How to deal with customers – the ABC International way*". Now link the customer/employer real need and the key feature with the phrase "which means that" and turn it into a benefit for customer/employer.

> "During both our induction and retraining pro-grammes I show our corporate video, *How to Deal with Customers – the ABC International Way*, **which means that** every new and existing staff member who attends my training course has a full understanding of our customer service culture."

At this stage of your commercial you should have engaged your prospect and demonstrated how you can satisfy one of their key needs. You can now move to cement your personal brand by showing that you can, in fact, **exceed** their needs.

Step 5 – You Excel At This is your **unique value proposition** and it should link back to your customer's/employer's need. At this point you are showing how you add real value to your customer/employer. You are now positioning your brand as adding value and making sure it stands out from the crowd for all the right reasons. This is where you hit the "I must buy it now" customer's/employer's button. You have aroused their interest and now you are galvanising them into action. This part of your personal commercial reinforces the message that you are the best at what you do. It tells your customer/employer what you excel at and that you believe in excellence.

This is where you hit the "I must buy it now" customer's/employer's button.

In the sample personal commercial it would be as follows:

> "I, like you, place a huge importance on customer service and that is why when I took responsibility for the up-skilling programme I commissioned a tailored video to illustrate to all staff the company's

vision to have the best customer service record in our market sector. It is my belief that we now set the standards when it comes to customer service and as a result we have grown our market share."

This final part of your commercial can demonstrate your winning qualities. It shows how you are in step with senior management, that you have the vision to see the bigger corporate picture, can get things done and set new standards. This is a very powerful message that will set your personal brand apart.

The finished commercial

"Hi, I'm Sean and I work in our Training and Development Academy as a senior consultant with responsibilities for improving the performance of all staff. I specialise in rapidly up-skilling new and existing employees to ABC's high performance standards. This ensures that departments like yours do not suffer loss of productivity or a reduction in customer service during staff changes.

What do you look for when a staff member joins your team from a training prospective?

So, am I right in saying that you place a huge importance on your staff understanding the principles of good customer care?

That's good to hear, because during both our induction and training programme I show our corporate video on "*How to Deal with Customers – the ABC International Way*", which means that every new and existing staff member who attends my training course has a full understanding of our customer service culture.

I, like you, place a strong emphasis on customer service and that is why when I took responsibility for the up-skilling programme I commissioned a tailored video to illustrate to all staff the company's vision to have the best customer service record in our market sector. It is my belief that we now set the standards when it comes to customer service and as a result we have grown our market share."

The aim of your commercial

Like all successful advertising campaigns, the main aim of your personal commercial is to sell your services to your target market by making them aware of what you do and how you add value to them. Your commercial is also focused on promoting your personal brand.

And, there are other benefits of a well-structured commercial. You will always be ready to answer compellingly when asked "what do you do?" Your reply will be consistent and benefit-focused. You appear professional, passionate and motivated. You and your brand become a highly desirable package. Selling yourself and promoting your brand is easy once you are prepared and well-practised.

It is also worth noting that your personal commercial should be remembered for all the right reasons. Everyone can name a TV commercial that was brilliantly made and entertaining, but were unable to remember the product it was supposed to be selling. Ensure your commercial stands out from the crowd by being both colourful and memorable in communicating your message.

Like all successful advertising campaigns, the main aim of your personal commercial is to sell your services to your target market by making them aware of what you do and how you add value to them. Your commercial is also focused on promoting your personal brand.

Three Ways to Script your "Commercial"

- Use bullet points at first, as this will overcome blank page syndrome. Expand your points when required
- Know your FAB (Features, Assets and Benefits) and use "which means that"
- Display your UVP (Unique Value Proposition)

Display your UVP (Unique Value Proposition)

Create a poster of your unique value proposition in order to maintain your positive mindset. Keep it colourful and attractive and have fun doing it. In the centre of the poster display your brand statement. Surround this with the qualities from your desirable factor file. Use pictures from magazines, bright colours and inspiring quotes to illustrate the essential messages. Highlight the key words as this will help train your brain to use these words when talking to your customers/employer.

Create a poster of your unique value proposition in order to maintain your positive mindset.

The "Dating Game"

Now that you are confident that you know what your customer/employer wants and expects from you, it is time to start building yourself up for the all-important meeting. You have a personal brand to sell and it won't sell itself. You need to leave your safe surroundings of doing nothing and get out into the real world and take some risks. Whether you are unemployed and are looking for a new job, or you have a job but want a more interesting or better paid one, the chances are the jobs won't come to you. You have to hunt them down and grab them. Transfer the principles of selling into the business of selling your career and you can start to appreciate the similarities.

You need to leave your safe surroundings of doing nothing and get out into the real world and take some risks.

Start to set up meetings with potential customers/ employers. The best jobs are rarely advertised, so you need to seek them out. Broaden your understanding of how to find a job. Every one of your competitors will look at the newspapers or place their CV with a recruitment agency in the hope of finding a job. Use alternative ways of finding work. Use your sales skills to generate work leads: targeted cold calling, traditional networking and networking Websites. Whatever method you use set up as many meetings as possible and learn something from each interview.

The best jobs are rarely advertised, so you need to seek them out.

Selling involves a degree of flirting so attending an external job interview is a bit like going on a blind date. They don't know you and you don't know them. After hours of preparation you set off looking your best. You hope they will be seduced by your charms and that they will embrace you with open arms. You meet each other for the first time full of enthusiasm, but with a degree of caution as you are reluctant to build up your hopes too much. Your desire is to build a long and lasting relationship.

Attending an external job interview is a bit like going on a blind date.

Sadly, there are more rejections than happy endings when it comes to blind dates, and interviews are no different. In today's climate there are more people available for work than there are suitors. The odds are stacked against you most of the time, so you need to improve those odds by projecting your best image. You need to look desirable in every way.

Equally, going to an **internal job interview** has its challenges. It's a bit like dating a friend; they know lots about you, but not everything. However, there are greater risks attached to dating your friend because if the liaison doesn't work out, the friendship could be damaged forever. People often undersell themselves in internal interviews by taking certain things for granted. They assume the boss knows them and the reasons why they would add value to the team. Far too often this is not the case and the impression that is created is that they are not as passionate about the relationship as they should be. They fail to tell their boss that they really want the job and that they have what it takes to make the relationship work. Once again, there are far more rejections than happy endings.

Job interviews, like dates, are fraught with dangers and anxieties. You may have to deal with many rejections before you find true romance. Once you find it, the relationship could last a lifetime, or you may fall out of love and have to start the process all over again. Remember, the key to happiness is to have fun trying to find your true lover or job. Rekindle the fire if your job has become boring and passionless. Always go to an interview oozing confidence. You get one chance to make that first impression; ensure that it is memorable for all the right reasons. Walk into the interview, whether it is internal or external, with a self-assurance and confidence that will blow your interviewer away. Then walk away and leave a winning last impression.

Selling successfully is about preparation; knowing that what you have to offer is what your customer requires. Unfortunately, one of the greatest weaknesses for most job candidates, whether it is an internal or external interview, is poor or even no preparation. Those who bother with preparation very often carry out only minimum research, relying on impromptu general answers that are vague and sometimes not even relevant to the job specifications. They turn up at the interview failing to look their best, apathy written all over their face, and they wonder why their name and the word "rejection" are used so often in the same sentence. Despite the fact that they probably had what it takes to be successful, they failed to deliver when it mattered – at the

Going to an internal job interview is a bit like dating a friend; they know lots about you, but not everything. However, there are greater risks attached to dating your friend because if the liaison doesn't work out, the friendship could be damaged forever.

Selling successfully is about preparation; knowing that what you have to offer is what your customer requires.

interview. They lack style and confidence, and it is simply unprofessional.

Thorough preparation is vital for peaking at the right moment. Top athletes fine tune their bodies so that they are in peak condition on the day of their most important event. They develop a routine over the years, often with the help of their coach. Their coach ensures that they stick to the agreed schedule and reviews each part of the game plan meticulously.

Being the best comes through hard work and preparation. You must develop a plan and use it in the days leading up to an important interview. Enlist the help of a family member or friend who will act as your coach.

"Success comes from knowing that you did your best to become the best that you are capable of becoming."
John Wooden, considered by many to be the greatest basketball coach in U.S. history

Research the job on offer

If you are going for an external interview gather as much information as you can about the company and job on offer and review it thoroughly.

If you are going for an external interview gather as much information as you can about the company and job on offer and review it thoroughly. Fill in any gaps in your research by talking to as many people as possible who are experts on the industry and market in which you work. Review the job specifications and main responsibilities as these will give you vital clues to the type of questions you might be asked. It also helps you to decide if this job is really for you. Going to job interviews just because you are desperate for work, or for a change, is not a good strategy as you will end up doing work that you don't like and that you don't do well. Over time, this will put you at a great disadvantage when the job that you really want comes around.

Going to job interviews just because you are desperate for work, or for a change, is not a good strategy as you will end up doing work that you don't like and that you don't do well.

Equally, if it is an internal position you are after, you shouldn't underestimate the preparation involved. Although you will be familiar with the company itself you still need to research fully the job on offer and your potential boss to understand their needs.

Evaluate your skills audit (see **Chapter 5**) and link your assets to the job. You must talk about these key skills during the interview. It's selling time. You must be able to demonstrate how your assets will benefit your potential customer/employer. Always talk about what you have to offer them from their perspective. Don't list endless achievements and skills if they don't relate to the job on offer. Also if you have any significant skills gaps, plan your strategy for dealing with potential tough questions. Look at ways of turning any potential negative answer into a positive one or think about how you could reduce the impact of any negative answers. Don't hope that they won't ask the tough question, because they will. Remember, hope is not a strategy. It's best to deal with how you answer difficult questions before the interview while you are clear-headed.

> Don't hope that they won't ask the tough question, because they will. Remember, hope is not a strategy.

Questions and answers

An interview is not just about answering questions; it is about selling yourself with carefully prepared, stand-out answers. Part of your research should include listing all the questions that you anticipate being asked. Plan your seductive answers. Practise these answers over and over again. Get your interview coach to practise with you. Selling is about confidence and knowing your product.

A simple but worthwhile exercise is to write down the three reasons why you are the best candidate for the job. Link these reasons to the job specification and then back them up with proof. Don't keep your three best attributes a secret – think of ways of talking about these qualities during the interview and highlight them at every opportunity.

> Write down the three reasons why you are the best candidate for the job.

A revealing question often asked is: "what were your key responsibilities in your last job and what did you actually achieve during your time there?" The responsibilities and achievements must be real and verifiable. Show what you have done and not what you would have done, if given the chance. You need to demonstrate that you are the best candidate and that your performance to date will prove that.

A clever interviewee links their achievements to their responsibilities and ensures that they speak about them in the context of the job on offer. They outline how their achievements would add value to the customer/employer. Be prepared to talk about successful projects that you were involved in, paying particular attention to your responsibilities within

> A clever interviewee links their achievements to their responsibilities and ensures that they speak about them in the context of the job on offer.

the projects. Highlight all the details that you expect the interviewer will be interested in.

Remember, no matter what questions are asked at an interview, the main answer that you must give throughout the interview is that you are the most suitable candidate in terms of skills, knowledge and expertise and that you are also the best candidate in terms of personality. You have the right attitude and a determination to be successful. That is the message that must be sent at all times throughout your interview. Your interview is where your personal brand comes alive and sells you.

Take a trip

If the location of your interview is new to you it is worthwhile visiting it and familiarising yourself with the building, and room, if possible. Check how long it took you to get there, if parking is available and whether it is possible to book a space. Find out how many people will be interviewing you. Get their details and any information that might help, such as their names and titles. Ensure that you have the correct spelling and pronunciation of their names. You don't want them to be correcting you at the start of your interview – it is off-putting for all concerned.

Dress to Impress

Decide on what you will wear to the interview well in advance. Have it cleaned and hanging in your wardrobe. Choose your outfit carefully as this forms part of your essential first impression. If it is an internal interview, show off something that you don't normally wear. Dress for the position that you are seeking.

Being well-presented sends out a desirable message: I'm ready, are you? Walk through that door flaunting your confidence and professionalism. The interview is your showcase.

Your pitch for the dream job

When you attend an interview, remember that, although you can't control the questions that will be asked, you can control the message you send through your personalised commercial. You can decide when it should be aired during the interview, allowing for maximum impact. Think of your winning qualities as forming the main picture board to your commercial for the job. An interview is just another media where your commercial can be aired.

> "You can have brilliant ideas, but if you can't get them across, your ideas won't get you anywhere."
> Legendary car manufacturer,
> Lee Iacocca

Cold-calling for an interview

As mentioned earlier, you need to broaden the methods that you use to get an interview. In the film *The Pursuit of Happyness* Will Smith gives a brilliant performance depicting the real-life rags-to-riches story of Chris Gardner. With no job prospects, Gardner relentlessly pursued an unpaid internship programme in a stock-broking firm. He cold-called the office and, finally, got an interview. Penniless and left to survive on the streets with his young son, he successfully completed his internship and was awarded a position within the firm. He went on to set up his own brokerage company and become extremely successful. Nobody handed Chris Gardner a job, he went after it with passion and determination despite the extreme circumstance that he found himself in.

Top Interview Tips

- Telephone to confirm your attendance and enthusiasm
- Arrive early
- Review your key notes
- Fresh breath and smell attractive
- Clean hands and nails
- Stand tall
- Smile and firm handshake
- Maintain good eye contact
- No jokes
- Be ready
- Sell yourself and your assets
- Show how you add value
- Ask for the job on offer

Cold-calling is a difficult sales method for even the best sales person but, used correctly, it can be used to open doors for finding work. Think of cold-calling as the start of your networking process. It is part of your research into establishing what is available and the beginning of forming real relationships.

In order to improve your chances of securing an interview from cold-calling, you must carry out some initial research on your target. Refrain from aimlessly making phone calls that interrupt people. Research the industry and how the company is performing. Talk to people working there to see if you can establish what they look for in their staff. Get a job description for the department of the company to which your services apply.

Before you pick up the phone or call to the office of your target company, you need to personalise your opening statement. Think about what value you can deliver to them. You will have only a minute to grab your potential customer's/ employer's attention. You need to be able to demonstrate that it is worth their time talking to you further.

Downsizing is another word for opportunity

It's 4 o'clock on a bright and sunny Friday afternoon. You have been working long and exhausting hours to ensure your latest project comes in on time. You have spent the last three weekends in the office going through endless reports. Your social life is on hold. This weekend is different – you're free. You've organised a few days away. Life is wonderful. Your career is progressing.

Just as you are about to leave your boss calls you into his/ her office. The message is short and very clear. Your company is downsizing due to the recession. You are the unlucky one who is being made redundant; your job is forfeited. The usual excuses are wheeled out to try and soften the blow. Unfortunately, this is a grim reality that many of us face at some stage in our careers.

Redundancy is seen by most people as a disaster, certainly not as an opportunity. For many people, their relationship with their job is similar to their love life. Initially, they do everything they can to impress. They dress well, are enthusiastic and very attentive. All is well in the garden of love. Gradually, over time, complacency sets in and even the most talented and driven people can develop an employee mindset and start to take things for granted. There is no longer a need to perform to their peak, update their skills or be thankful for their pay cheque. Then, when the break-up happens it usually hits them the hardest. They didn't see it coming and they find it very hard to believe that they now are unemployed. They are not equipped to move on and start again.

When was the last time you … ?

- Reviewed your CV and updated it with your current skills and job experience?
- Had it professionally typed and presented?
- Showed it to a professional recruiter, and asked their advice?
- Gave a copy to your HR manager to update their records?
- Read your CV and assured yourself, based on the information contained in it, that you have the right credentials for the type of work that appeals to you?
- Turned your CV into a personal brochure outlining the benefits of hiring you?

Employees who are made redundant can often see themselves as victims for far too long. All they see is doom and gloom and they miss most of the opportunities that redundancy can bring. Redundancy is an opportunity to progress your career, to stretch your skills and knowledge. It's an opportunity to grow and become innovative in seeking new work. If the traditional five-day-a-week job is not available look at other avenues that are open to you. Think about working for more than one customer/employer. There might not be a five-day job available but there could be a one- or two-day a week job opening up. Build up your portfolio of customers/employers. Over time this may prove to be more secure than the traditional five-day-a-week, one customer/employer type of job.

> "When you reach an obstacle, turn it into an opportunity. You have the choice. You can overcome and be a winner, or you can allow it to overcome you and be a loser. The choice is yours and yours alone. Refuse to throw in the towel. Go that extra mile that failures refuse to travel. It is far better to be exhausted from success than to be rested from failure."
>
> Mary Kay Ash, founder of Mary Kay Cosmetics

Plenty more fish in the sea

Always remember that *you* haven't been made redundant – your *job* has. As soon as you receive your notice, it's time to start getting noticed again. Buy yourself a new suit, get a new hairstyle, take a holiday, recharge your batteries and refocus your mind. Discard any negative baggage before you go looking for work. Send out the message: "Hi, I'm available". Get yourself back in the market. Be positive and act like a true leader.

> Always remember that *you* haven't been made redundant – your *job* has.

> "The pessimist complains about the wind. The optimist expects it to change. The leader adjusts the sails."
>
> John Maxwell

Do's and Don'ts of the Marketing Department – Protect Your Personal Brand

DO:
- ✓ **Be a Master**
- ✓ Decide that your career is important and you are prepared to work hard at being exceptional.
- ✓ Intentionally position yourself for success through your desirable brand.
- ✓ Create a commercial that appeals to your target market.
- ✓ Build your summary position by explaining what your brand offers, who your target audience is and show proof to support the benefits of dealing with you.

✓ Bring passion to your pursuit of employability.
✓ Design your CV as a personal brochure.
✓ Broaden your methods of finding work.

DON'T:

☒ **Don't Be a Slave**

☒ Don't become a self-obsessed attention-seeker and confuse this with personal branding.

☒ Don't make false claims about your abilities.

☒ Don't fall victim to redundancy and fail to see the opportunities.

☒ Don't lose heart when your first interview does not go well.

☒ Don't undersell your benefits.

☒ Don't forget to sell benefits and not features.

If you don't **get noticed** for all the right reasons, it's likely you will receive your **notice**.

Apply one new idea every week to become more employable and successful.

PERSONAL THOUGHTS

What will I do differently tomorrow?

CHAPTER 5

RESEARCH & DEVELOPMENT: PERSONAL DEVELOPMENT AND UNDERSTANDING YOUR TRUE VALUE

Quick guide to this chapter

- Become exceptional at what you do
- Always seek out ways to improve
- Why do you need a customer/employer care strategy?
- Link your customer/employer care strategy to your personal development plan
- SWOT analysis report
- How can you use your strengths to take advantage of the opportunities that you have identified?
- Conduct a skills audit – your skills bank is your future.
- Your guide to the Four-Step Skills Audit Method
- Invest in your assets
- How valuable are your assets?
- How to create your personal development plan
- Continued investment in your assets

Be exceptional at what you do

In order for business leaders to grow their companies successfully, they need the economies in which they operate to be successful. Successful economies are those with companies that can rapidly adapt to the changing global environment. Successful companies have people who can also adapt to this environment. As a result, to be employable in today's job market you need a new way of thinking and behaving.

Companies in every industry need people who can adapt quickly and positively to change. Success requires people to stop thinking like employees and start behaving like entrepreneurs. Being an entrepreneur in the workplace means being flexible, visionary and always being on the lookout for opportunities to improve the way you work. Entrepreneurs in the workplace seek excellence and ways to add real value to the business. They don't believe that anyone owes them an income; they must go out and earn it for themselves.

When you look around your own workplace you will notice that most people want to be **good** at what they do. As employees they are conditioned to be **good**. Their work environment is set up so that they can be **good** performers. Their boss is happy with a **good** performance from them. Thus, there is no surprise that when you look at the results of performance reviews, the vast majority of employees receive a **good** rating.

However, this acceptance of performing at a good standard is not healthy if you want to stay employable. There is a growing disconnection between the level of performance that is required to succeed in today's economic climate and that which employees tend to deliver. And it is not the underperforming employees that are the cause of this disconnect. It is caused by employees who settle for being good and are content to receive a good rating. As the vast majority of employees receive a "good rating" then it can be argued that "good" is now used to describe a minimum level of acceptable performance.

But being good at your job is no longer good enough. Being an employee and displaying an employee mindset is no longer good enough. If your goal is to be employable, then you must always seek **excellence**. You need to excite your customer/employer by exceeding their expectation, by bringing your performance level to new heights.

There is also a practical and economic reason why you

Entrepreneurs in the workplace seek excellence and ways to add real value to the business. They don't believe that anyone owes them an income; they must go out and earn it for themselves.

"Good" is now used to describe a minimum level of acceptable performance.
But being good at your job is no longer good enough.

need your performance to excel: the best way to achieve your ambition of being employable is to focus on ensuring that your customer/employer earns enough money to pay your wages. The simple business reality that "good performers" often overlook is that if your customer/employer doesn't make money then it is unlikely that you will.

the best way to achieve your ambition of being employable is to focus on ensuring that your customer/employer earns enough money to pay your wages

Excellence requires effort

The difficulty with having entrepreneurial commitment is that it requires hard work. Excellence doesn't happen just because you want it to happen; it needs a well-devised strategy and continuous improvement. Tiger Woods isn't the greatest golfer in the world because of his talent alone. He is the greatest because he is constantly looking at ways to improve his talents. He seeks out excellence in every aspect of his game. He realises that if he stands still then his rivals will one day overtake him. The key for Tiger is to continually develop and improve his game. Despite being number one in world rankings, he knows he can be better.

To move forward successfully you need to make a decision. Do you want to remain a good employee with a good performance record and still risk losing your job, or become an outstanding performer, someone who makes a difference by embracing excellence? In **Chapter 3** we confronted the fact that is vital for your continued employability that you provide a consistently high level of performance together with a service that exceeds your customer's/employer's needs. This requires excellence; it requires you to complete your work at a level of excellence all of the time. You need to give more and ask more of yourself than your customer/employer might ask of you.

American entrepreneur Debbi Fields, founder of Mrs Fields Cookies, believes in excellence: "The important thing is not being afraid to take a chance. Remember, the greatest failure is to not try. Once you find something you love to do, be the best at doing it."

Always seek out ways to improve

To achieve excellence requires a strategy for continuous improvement. The skills, knowledge and expertise that brought you this far in your career will not sustain your employability into the future. The competition for work will intensify and only the best, those that can deliver excellence to their customer/employer on a regular basis, will survive.

In sport, top performers work hard at gaining the edge over their rivals. They take responsibility for their performance. They realise that it is the finer details, and small improvements, that can be the difference between winning and coming second. The Irish rugby pundit and ex-player, Conor O'Shea, describes what it takes to be the best when talking about the Irish Grand Slam winning team of 2009:

> "When all is said and done rugby is about taking responsibility. Winning teams have leaders who are willing to put their necks on the line, who always put their hands up and say 'I'll do the job'."

He goes on to talk about team captain, Brian O'Driscoll's, extraordinary efforts. "His try was all about inches and it is inches that make the difference. The man is incredible."

Excellence is about making small improvements consistently. Brian Tracy, a leading authority on the development of human potential, believes that "[t]he key to long-term success is for you to dedicate yourself to continuous improvement." He also talks about the cumulative effect:

> "If you become one tenth of 1% more productive each day, that amounts to one half of 1% more productive each week. One half of 1% more productive each week amounts to 2% more productive each month and 26% more productive each year. The cumulative effect of becoming a tiny bit better and more productive amounts to a tremendous increase in your value and your output over time."

This level of improvement is achievable. You can become exceptional, not overnight, but over time. You need a "can-do" attitude to produce winning results consistently. Winners not only believe that they can produce excellence, they go out and produce excellent performances even in the toughest conditions. Excuses are not an option.

"If you become one tenth of 1% more productive each day, that amounts to one half of 1% more productive each week. One half of 1% more productive each week amounts to 2% more productive each month and 26% more productive each year. The cumulative effect of becoming a tiny bit better and more productive amounts to a tremendous increase in your value and your output over time."

Brian Tracy

"The winners in life think constantly in terms of I can, I will, and I am. Losers, on the other hand, concentrate their waking thoughts on what they should have or would have done, or what they can't do."

Dennis Waitley, author of *The Psychology of Winning*

Show your caring side

Many of the skills, knowledge and experience that you have developed over the years may no longer be sought after, and some will even have become obsolete. The challenge is to stay marketable in the future. This means that you need to adapt to new roles and the changing needs of your customer/employer. Now more than ever it makes sense to invest time in building your career and improving your prospects of employment.

Although companies need to adapt to the changing business environment, they must also look after their customers. They prosper because they continually ask their customers what they need and then give it to them. However, during the boom years many businesses lost sight of this basic principle. They stopped caring about their customers and as a result many customers fell out of love with them. And such was the plentiful supply of customers that these businesses didn't even notice that their loyal customers were going elsewhere. Today it is a different story, as many businesses are finding to their cost. Dissatisfied customers have left them and are unlikely to return, and as a consequence the lost revenue is now having a major impact on their survival plans.

You are no different. You need to look after your customer/employer the way you look after your external customers. You need to understand their current as well as future requirements. Show your love by exceeding their needs. Unfortunately, most employees think of their customer's/employer's current needs and do not invest enough time or resources developing themselves to meet their customer's/employer's **future** needs. As a result, their service can become outdated and even obsolete. Part of the process of ensuring that you don't go out of fashion is to introduce a winning customer/employer care strategy.

Although companies need to adapt to the changing business environment, they must also look after their customers.

during the boom years many businesses lost sight of this basic principle

You need to look after your customer/employer the way you look after your external customers.

Why do you need a customer/employer care strategy?

Your customer care strategy should also outline your commitment to putting your customer/employer at the centre of everything that you do. When it comes to delivering excellence, there is no place for thinking like an employee. Never lose sight of the fact that you are dependent on your customer/employer for your financial well being. Therefore, when you receive your wages take a little time to consider why your customer/employer is paying you and whether your level of performance ensures that they will pay you again next month?

Every time your customer/employer comes into contact with you, they form an opinion of you. Over time, this creates an image of your personal brand and the value that you provide. This ultimately affects your business relationship and whether they want to continue to buy your services. A strong relationship is built when your customer/employer is confident that the level of performance they receive from you is what they expect *and more.*

Fulfilling your employer's current and future needs is essential for your career survival. If you don't, someone else will quickly fill your shoes. Focusing your energies on exceeding these needs will move your career forward. Your customer care strategy should reflect this.

At this stage of your journey you have already established your customer's/employer's needs and wants by carrying out a detailed needs analysis. You are aware of your critical impact points and you are keenly aware of the importance of exceeding these requirements. However, what procedures have you put in place to monitor whether you are consistently exceeding the performance levels required by your customer/employer?

Every time your customer/employer comes into contact with you, they form an opinion of you.

Fulfilling your employer's current and future needs is essential for your career survival. If you don't, someone else will quickly fill your shoes.

Feedback on your customer/employer care strategy

Measure your excellence; put some measurement tools in place to judge your progress. When you finish a project or an important piece of work, have a debriefing session with your boss. Look for feedback on your performance. Simple questions such as "next time, how could I improve the service that I give you?" or "is there anything that you would like me to do differently next time?" will provide you with useful information. Listen carefully to the feedback, and then act on that information.

Look for feedback on your performance.

From time to time your customer/employer will volunteer some critical feedback on your performance. Never view this feedback as a personal attack on your performance and don't become defensive and argue with them or try to explain yourself. Thank them for their comments. If you disagree with their view, ask them for some examples to support their opinion. This may clarify their viewpoint for you and allow you to make the required changes.

Linking your customer/employer care strategy to your personal development plan

Ask yourself how you have invested in your customer/employer care strategy. In a dynamic jobs market, how you answer this question could save you a lot of wasted learning and development time. Detailed customer/employer information is vital. Careful research here will give you the edge. It will allow you to concentrate on improving the key areas that will differentiate you from your competitors. You have carried out various pieces of quality research to date; you know what is expected from you; now, can you deliver?

Detailed customer/employer information is vital. Careful research here will give you the edge. It will allow you to concentrate on improving the key areas that will differentiate you from your competitors.

Use the template below to link your findings to your personal development plan. Aside from the information that you currently possess you may also establish some new data to help you.

Employability Needs Analysis		
	Questions	**Findings**
Future Opportunities	• What are your customer's/ employer's future plans? • Which departments in your organisation seem likely to expand? • Where is the money being invested? • Which manager continues to develop his or her staff? • What area will be in demand five years from now? • What new services are being designed?	
Growth Areas	• What part of the business is growing? • What part of the business is most profitable? • How could you add value to a growth area? • Where is the future growth potential? • What are customers looking for more of? • What business units are hiring additional staff?	
New Markets	• What markets are currently underdeveloped? • Can your customer/employer break into these markets? • Which manager has the vision to deliver in these new markets? • What skills would you need to work in these markets? • What have you to offer these new markets?	

New Products	<ul><li>What new products are being developed?</li><li>What new products need to be developed?</li><li>How can you help with this project?</li><li>What impact will the new product have on your job?</li><li>What have you to offer?</li></ul>	
Technology	<ul><li>What type of technology is required to maintain profitability?</li><li>How can you help?</li><li>What impact will new technology have on your current job?</li></ul>	
Competitors	<ul><li>What are your competitors' strategies to remain employable?</li><li>Who are your up-and-coming competitors?</li><li>What are they doing to gain greater brand exposure and recognition?</li><li>What skills and knowledge do they have that you are lacking?</li></ul>	
Main Priorities	<ul><li>What are your core skills and work activities?</li><li>Will they still be a priority to your customer/employer in the medium- to long-term?</li><li>What area must you develop to remain employable?</li><li>How adaptable are you?</li></ul>	
Skill Requirements	<ul><li>What does your skills audit tell you?</li><li>What new skills will your customer/employer need in the future?</li><li>Where are the key skills' shortages?</li><li>Which of your skills are transferable?</li><li>How can your skills add value to your customer/employer?</li><li>How quickly can you up-skill?</li></ul>	

Now you need to convert this raw research data into the skills and knowledge that your customer/employer will require over the next few years, and this will be a crucial part of your plan for your future employability. Your research should form the basis of your medium- to long-term business development strategy. It will also highlight any areas where you might require up-skilling, new knowledge or new competencies.

In **Chapter 4** we examined how you can develop your personal brand based on your main strengths, your personality and your assets. However, for your personal brand to succeed over the long-term, your qualities must be aligned to your customer's/employer's future needs. By doing this you will be in a strong position to maximise your brand's value. Now that you fully understand your customer's/employer's needs, it is worth exploring your offerings a little further at this point.

There are a few factors to keep in mind before you dash off and start to write up your personal development plan. First, conduct a "**SWOT analysis**". This is a simple exercise whereby you outline your **S**trengths and **W**eaknesses, together with the **T**hreats and **O**pportunities that you will encounter. Your strengths will give you a clear understanding of your employment opportunities, whereas any weaknesses in your personal development plan can cause threats to your employability.

These questions require honest and blunt answers in order to make this exercise as beneficial as possible for you. Once you have completed a bit of soul searching and have gathered all of this information, organise it into a SWOT analysis report which follows.

To help you understand how the SWOT analysis method could work for you, review the checklist set out below:

Conduct a "SWOT analysis" – a simple exercise whereby you outline your Strengths and Weaknesses, together with the Threats and Opportunities that you will encounter

Personal SWOT Analysis	
Strengths	**Weaknesses**
• What do you excel at? • What differentiates you from your potential competitors? • Why do your customers/employers keep coming back to you? • What are you main personal brand attributes? • What are your top three skills? • How strong is your personal network of contacts?	• Have you got the skills required to exceed your customer/employer needs? • Are you truly flexible? • Can you easily adapt to change? • Have you got an employee mindset? • How much energy do you have? • Are you a hard worker without vision? • What does your customer/employer see as a weakness in you? • Do others outperform you?
Opportunities	**Threats**
• What future opportunities are available for you in the jobs market? • What type of work have you spotted that your competitors have missed? • Where are the gaps that you are proposing to fill? • What are the new markets that require your skills and knowledge? • What "green shoots" have you unearthed?	• Have your competitors more to offer than you? • Will the skills and knowledge that you currently provide become obsolete soon? • Have you invested enough in your training and development needs? • Will the new work practices accommodate your mindset? • Have you become stuck in your comfort zone? • What essential skills are missing from your skills bank?

SWOT analysis report		
Factors	**Internal**	**External**
Positive	**Strengths**	**Opportunities**
	• Your experience and what you excel at • Your skills • Your knowledge	• Gap in the market • New market and green shoots • New needs
Negative	**Weaknesses**	**Threats**
	• Lack of experience • Skills' shortage • Employee mindset characteristics	• Competition • Lack of training and development • Changing work market • Essential skills missing from skills bank

How can you use your strengths to take advantage of the opportunities that you have identified?

Your personal SWOT analysis report clearly outlines your current position. It acts as an executive summary for your business. The next step is to use this data strategically and with a clear vision. Good information is essential, but how you use it is what makes it powerful.

Missed opportunities are wasteful and largely avoidable. Developing your entrepreneurial way of thinking helps you to seek out the options available. Improving your employability grows out of two interrelated elements:

Improving your employability grows out of two interrelated elements:

• What you have to offer
• Your customer's/employer's needs

• What you have to offer
• Your customer's/employer's needs.

From the information you have collected about yourself, compare what you have to offer with your customer's/employer's needs. Do they match? Are you talking the same language? If your customer/employer needs flexibility does it match your definition of flexibility? Their definition might be that they expect you to work in any department depending on work volumes, while you believe you are flexible because you can take your lunch-break at any time. Clearly, there is a mismatch here.

Completing this exercise requires you to dig deep into each need of your customer/employer and to honestly assess if there is a gap between it and your ability to meet that need. This is another vital stage of your journey to sustainable employment. The gaps that you have exposed here need to be addressed in your personal development plan. This process will put you in a healthy position to avail of future opportunities.

Business assets – your skills bank

The last step to undertake before you write your personal development plan (PDP) is to evaluate your skills bank. Part of a winning PDP is to review all of your skills, and not just the ones that you are missing or you feel are weak. Sometimes it is your strong skills that will require further development in order to stay competitive.

Review all of your skills, and not just the ones that you are missing or you feel are weak. Sometimes it is your strong skills that will require further development in order to stay competitive.

When people are asked to list their skills, a small list is usually produced. Most take a very narrow approach and think that the only worthwhile skills they possess are the ones they currently use in their job. Remember, your skills are your business assets and **every** skill you have adds value. When determining what should be included in your skills bank, you need to broaden your view and understanding of what constitutes a skill.

Work practices and the technology you use are constantly changing. Some of the skills that you have developed are already outdated, while the need for new skills is constantly emerging. Also the average person now requires a greater range of skills to meet their customer's/employer's needs. The greater number of skills in your skills bank, the greater number of options are open to you. You also need to consider the skills that you have mastered over the years that are transferable. These may not be obvious immediately so it's worth spending some time reflecting on all of your skills. Carrying out a skills audit will give you a complete picture of what you have to offer your customer/employer in terms of skills, knowledge and expertise.

Carrying out a skills audit will give you a complete picture of what you have to offer your customer/employer in terms of skills, knowledge and expertise.

Conduct a skills audit

Your future employability will be dependent on your ability to recognise the skills you use and which skills add value to your customer/employer. Companies are willing to pay a premium for people with the skills that they can't do without. It is your responsibility to develop these priceless assets.

Taking time out to compile a comprehensive inventory of all your skills is vital if you want to:

Taking time out to compile a comprehensive inventory of all your skills is vital if you want to:

- stay competitive in a new dynamic business world
- promote yourself as a marketable and employable brand
- receive the true value of your asset bank
- improve your chances of using the skills you enjoy
- discover how flexible you can be
- break free from an employee mindset
- understand which skills are transferable

- stay competitive in a new dynamic business world
- promote yourself as a marketable and employable brand
- receive the true value of your asset bank
- improve your chances of using the skills you enjoy
- discover how flexible you can be
- break free from an employee mindset
- understand which skills are transferable

To avoid the trap of taking some of your skills for granted, or only looking at your abilities in the workplace, you should write down your skills in all areas of your life. The skills you use at work only represent a portion of your overall abilities. You need to broaden your view of your skills bank, consider skills you employ at home, including hobbies and voluntary work, and then list them all under the following seven headings:

Skills' Register	
Skills	**Examples**
Full-Time Work Skills	Networking
	Ability to learn
	Reliability
	Innovating
	Punctuality
	Business writing
	Telephone manner
	Delegating
	Problem-solving
	Prioritising
	Reporting
	Time management
	Specific job skills
People Skills	Relationship building
	Leadership
	Interpersonal
	Inspiring
	Influencing
	Team working
	Verbal communication
	Written communication
	Questioning skills
	Evaluating replies to questions
	Ability to answer questions
	Listening
	Chairing meetings
	Involving people
	Participating at meetings
	Giving feedback
	Speaking clearly
	Persuading
	Being empathetic

Specialist Skills	Technical
	Languages
	Qualifications
	Experience
	Product knowledge
	IT skills
	Industry knowledge
	Project management
	Software packages
	Presenting
	Managerial
	Current job
General Skills	Controlling
	Financial understanding
	Adaptability
	Business acumen
	Accuracy
	Ability to work on own
	Setting goals
	Achieving goals
	Systematic
	Persistence
	Organising
	Research
	General knowledge
	Conversation
	Grooming
	Reading
	Writing
	Big picture view
Other Work Experience Skills	Part-time work
	Voluntary work
	Care in the community work
	Care in the home work
	Community work
	Previous work
	Committee work

Skills Learnt from Hobbies	Team hobbies
	Individual hobbies
	Evening classes
	Sports
Family Skills	Household budgeting
	Planning
	Logistical
	Conflicting roles
	Time management
	Multi-tasking
	Negotiating techniques
	Ability to communicate with people at different levels
	Managing relationships
	Driving
	Confidential
	Conciliation
	Sensitivity
	Keep up with trends
	School work
	Diplomacy
	Comforting
	Decision-making

Though the above list of approximately 100 skills is not exhaustive, it will give you a basis to work from. Some of the skills highlighted could be broken down further, such as leadership and questioning skills. To get the most from this exercise, don't limit yourself to using terms that can describe several skills, such as "managerial skills". List each skill individually. Also, refrain from getting too technical about the differences between skills and attributes. This is a **brainstorming activity**, similar to the one carried out for your personal branding. The more skills that you list, the greater competitive advantage you can achieve because you will have more to offer your customer/employer.

Once you have listed all of the skills that you possess in your skills bank, move to the next phase and carry out

> This is a brainstorming activity, similar to the one carried out for your personal branding. The more skills that you list, the greater competitive advantage you can achieve because you will have more to offer your customer/employer.

a detailed **skills audit**. This exercise will take some time to complete, but it is worthwhile as it will provide you with an assessment of your skills. This will then indicate how strong your position is compared to your competition and the skills they offer.

The Four-Step Skills Audit Method™

To get the best results from any audit requires a systematic approach. By going through the Four-Step Skills Audit Method™ you will ensure that you have a clear understanding of which of your skills will need further development and which ones are in a strong position. Use the Four-Step Skills Audit Method as follows:

1. Group the skills you have indentified through your SWOT analysis and in your skills bank analysis under the following five labels. Also from your SWOT analysis, identify any skills that are not currently in your skills bank, but which will feature prominently within the next two years, and include them.

Skills Analysis	
Skills Bank	**Grade**
(i) Work-related skills	
(ii) People skills	
(iii) Specialist skills	
(iv) General skills	
(v) Social skills	

2. Identify any training gap in your list by grading each skill as follows:

- **Fully Developed** (no further improvement is required during the next audit period)
- **Requires Improvement** (briefly describe the type of training required, e.g. haven't used the skill in a while so will need a refresher course
- **New skill development** – (briefly describe the type of training required, e.g. haven't used the skill before so will need beginners course)

3. Once you have determined which skills require improvement then prioritise them by forming a grid based on the following two axes:

- What adds value to my customer/employer?
- What skills do I enjoy using most?

Place each skill in its appropriate place. This step helps to highlight which skills you need to focus on developing.

Skills Priority Grid	
High Value Low Enjoyment P2	High Value High Enjoyment P1
Low Value Low Enjoyment P4	Low Value High Enjoyment P3

4. From P1 and P2 decide on the top three priority skills that require improvement, and add them to your personal development plan. These are the skills that will add most value to your customer/employer, so this is an important decision. Now invest your time wisely and commit to developing these skills.

Invest in your assets

Like any successful business you should invest in your assets, which are your skills and expertise.

Like any successful business you should invest in your assets, which are your skills and expertise. These need to be updated regularly; otherwise they may lose their value. This can be achieved by writing your **personal development plan**. Your personal development plan is a simple document that outlines what you need to do. It is your responsibility to write it and then implement it. That way you can devise any type of schedule that suits your requirements.

Investing in your skills can take many different forms. Training courses provided by your company, professional qualifications, learning from others, and reading are just some of the ways through which you can be proactive with your learning. You can also develop other skills through sporting activities, such as improving your leadership skills by managing your local kids' football team.

Monitor your progress

Monitoring your progress regularly keeps your development on track.

Monitoring your progress regularly keeps your development on track. At the end of each quarter you should carry out a quick personal development audit and review where you spent your time and money in developing your skills. This review, together with your analysis of your customer/employer needs, will provide you with clarity on what areas of development should be included in your plan.

Create a simple database to track all of your learning activities. This can be the beginning of a very simple development database. You will need to track such things as:

- The learning activities that you participated in
- The date of the activity
- What you learnt
- How it added value to you
- How much it cost
- Any positive comments about the learning activity (very practical training course and I got a chance to practise some skills)

- Any negative comment about the learning activity (didn't meet my objectives, waste of time attending)
- How much time I spent at learning activity

Also, include a list of the people whom you have learnt from. Think of ways to keep these people interested in your development so that they will continue to pass on their knowledge to you.

How valuable are your assets?

Any financial director will know how much their company's assets are worth. However, can you say how much your assets are worth? Never underestimate the real value of your assets as they will determine your employability. To borrow a phrase from MasterCard they are "Priceless".

The best insurance policy that you can take out to protect the value of your assets is your **personal development plan** (PDP). Always remain open to further development and learning new things; seek out opportunities to stretch yourself.

How to create your personal development plan

Your PDP will provide a coherent approach to your personal development. It is an essential document if you want to be employable. Without it, you are offering skills, knowledge and expertise that are required today but may be out of date next year if you don't keep them updated. Therefore your PDP should practically outline how you will achieve your development goals and what specific actions you need to take. An effective PDP will keep you focused on your key areas of improvement. The following five-step approach is a good model to use.

The benefits of investing in your personal development include:

- Improve your chances of being employable
- Be proactive about effecting change rather than being at the mercy of it
- Keep yourself focused on your career goals
- Get the best out of yourself
- Acquire more self-confidence and self belief in your abilities
- Master your skills
- Enhance your portfolio of skills, knowledge and expertise
- Increase your network of contacts
- Perform your work more efficiently
- Enhance your feelings of security through improved employability
- Build your flexibility within your organisation

5-Step Guide to Creating Your PDP

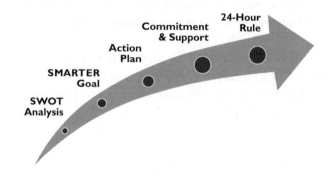

Step 1   SWOT analysis and skills audit

You have already taken the first step in this process by completing your SWOT analysis and skills audit. You have now established the skills that you need to work on so that you can excel in your work and remain employable. This is your **current position.**

Now, from your list of skills that require improvement, take your top three priority skills and work your way through the rest of this process and you will then end up at your preferred position.

Step 2   Set your SMARTER Goal

Writing down goals gives clarity and turns plans into reality. Sometimes the thought of learning a new skill can be daunting. If it is a large development goal, break it down into smaller objectives. Use the SMARTER Way™ discussed in **Chapter 3** to define each objective. Once these skills have been fully developed, you will be at your **preferred position.**

Step 3   Action plan

Having defined your development needs, draw up a detailed action plan to bridge the gap between your current position and your preferred position. The best way to begin this part of the process is to state the end result. Specify in detail your preferred position, paying particular attention to describing the skills that you are using. Next, work your way back to your current position by documenting each stage that you need to go through in order to arrive at your preferred position. Describe the type of training that took place, where you got a chance to practise the new skills and how long it took to get there. You have now completed your action plan.

Step 4   Gain commitment and support

All worthwhile improvements involve risk, commitment and persistence. Your personal development will require support from others and you need to identify, from the outset, who these people will be. For example, if you need time off for training, you need buy-in from your manager to your PDP. Show them how your PDP will benefit them and why it is important to you. Ask for their support.

All worthwhile improvements involve risk, commitment and persistence.

Step 5   The 24-hour rule

The 24-hour rule is extremely important as it galvanises you into action. After all your hard work in the research and planning stages, it is essential that you don't fail to take significant action towards achieving your goal(s) within 24 hours of having set them. The one simple principle behind every successfully completed goal is that you must *start*. As each day passes without any action taking place, the probability of the goal being completed successfully lessens, and by the end of the first week it is down to a 1 in 10 chance of being done. Therefore, begin any action link to your goal within the first 24 hours of setting the goal and your chance of successfully completing it is high. It doesn't matter whether the action is big or small because once you have started the process you are more likely to complete it.

The one simple principle behind every successfully completed goal is that you must *start*.

Monitor your journey

It is also important to monitor and record your development. This will make it easier to track your progress. When you have completed your development objective, you must hold a debriefing session with the people who were involved or supported your development. Establish some useful facts for your next development session such as:

- What worked well?
- What would you do differently next time?
- What feedback did you receive from your support people?

Continued investment in your assets

Your personal development plan is directly linked to your employability. Therefore, you need to focus on monitoring, measuring and continuous improvements. Your PDP is not a static document that you pick up once or twice a year. It involves a continuing investment, both in terms of time and learning.

"Sometimes you have to take a step or two back before you make a giant leap forward", explains Tiger Woods, who successfully reconstructed his game in order to reach new heights of performance.

Sometimes, after careful reflection on your PDP, you may need to take some hard decisions that could necessitate serious action. To others your decision may appear as if your career is taking a backward step. However, if you take the long-term view and link your PDP to the future needs of your customer/employer, the giant leap forward will bring great rewards.

The benefits of continuously developing your assets (skills bank) are not just confined to your customer/employer. You will also:

- realise your full potential
- improve your ability to deal with change
- acquire knowledge and learning agility
- build your personal brand and value
- increase your flexibility
- avail of career opportunities
- maintain your motivation to perform at the highest level

Tracking the Development of your Skills Bank				
Skills I Want to Develop	**How I Can Develop Them?**	**Action Points**	**Date**	**Support**
Networking	Join a networking group	Research local areas for different types of networking groups Attend an introduction meeting	By 1 October	Manager

Do's and Don'ts of your Research & Development department:
Your personal development strategy

DO:

- ✓ **Be a Master**
- ✓ Carry out a skills audit – know your assets
- ✓ Adapt your skills to meet your customer's/employer's needs
- ✓ Develop for the future – creates opportunities
- ✓ Invest in your skills
- ✓ Update your personal development plan on a regular basis
- ✓ Track and monitor your progress
- ✓ Research and understand the future needs of your customer/employer

DON'T:

- ☒ **Be a Slave**
- ☒ Don't believe that a career is for other people
- ☒ Don't allow a disparity between the level of performance that is required to move your business forward in today's economic climate, and the level of performance that you deliver
- ☒ Don't forget to update your customer/employer care strategy
- ☒ Don't limit the number of skills you possess
- ☒ Don't think of your PDP as a static document
- ☒ Don't waste time and resources developing skills that will become obsolete in the near future
- ☒ Don't ignore the 24-hour rule

Apply one new idea every week to become more employable and successful.

PERSONAL THOUGHTS

What will I do differently tomorrow?

CHAPTER 6

SALES: NETWORKING YOUR WAY TO SUCCESS

Quick guide to this chapter

- What is business networking?
- How career networking works
- Benefits of effective career networking
- Career networking professionally
- How to get the best out of your network
- How career networking can unearth hidden work opportunities
- How to grow your career network to find the hidden work gems
- You are networking all the time

What is business networking?

Effective business networking allows you to benefit from people you know to help you and your business. According to Dr Ivan Misner, founder and chairman of BNI, the world's largest business networking organisation:

> "Business networking is leveraging your business and personal connections to bring you a regular supply of new business."

"Business networking is leveraging your business and personal connections to bring you a regular supply of new business."

Dr Ivan Misner

Networking is about making the most out of your contacts in a professional and mutually beneficial way. It is not about just happening to know the right people, but rather getting the right people to know about you. It is a structured process that will unearth opportunities you may otherwise never have discovered.

Networking is not about just happening to know the right people, but rather getting the right people to know about you.

Networking involves building real relationships with fellow business people and potential customers/employers. It can be an extremely effective way of gathering information about people, their needs and whether they are interested in what you have to offer. Nevertheless, if done properly, it can be a slow process as, like most relationships, it takes time to build trust. Effective networking is not simply about attending meet-and-greet events, shaking hands and swapping business cards. It is not speed dating.

"You can close more business in two months by becoming interested in other people than you can in two years by trying to get people interested in you."
Dale Carnegie

Good networking is about reaching a larger number of people than you might otherwise, listening to see how you can help them and then asking the right questions to gather useful information. Networking helps you to further your career with your existing customer/employer by establishing yourself with the right people. A good network will provide you with additional resources to help you understand your business sector and how it works at a higher level. Leveraging these contacts to become involved in important work projects, committees and forums will enhance your employability. Never assume that your current customer/employer, and more specifically the right people within your organisation, know what you can offer and deliver to them.

Career networking

Never assume that your current customer/employer, and more specifically the right people within your organisation, know what you can offer and deliver to them.

Career networking is increasing the reach of your personal brand. It involves building meaningful relationships with people who can influence and support your career. In essence, it's no different to business networking. Your ability to draw on people you know to help you make decisions about your career development is an important skill in being successful and remaining employable. You are never more than four or five people away from the person who will make a real difference to your career. Always keep in mind that it's not what you know, it's not who you know, **it's who knows you and what you can do that counts**.

Always keep in mind that it's not what you know, it's not who you know, it's who knows you and what you can do that counts.

When networking for career and personal development you must find the right people to talk to and let them know what it is you want them to help you with. Don't jump in and start aimlessly talking to everyone about your career, or your need to find a new job. Each interaction with a contact must have a purpose.

Each interaction with a contact must have a purpose.

It is also important to constantly update and grow your network file. Break free from your comfort zone of dependable friends and acquaintances and include new people. You never know who can help you until you ask. And, seek out quality, not quantity.

Benefits of networking

Managing your career, looking for a job or trying to remain employable can be a lonely experience. Everyone needs support and guidance from time to time. It can be amazing to discover the kind of help that people you know can offer you. Broaden your circle of contacts and reap the rewards that effective networking can bring. It's my experience that you usually get the greatest help and guidance from the most unlikely of sources.

Below is a list of 10 reasons why networking is beneficial:

1. **Become better known** – for all the right reasons, such as displaying the right attitude in difficult times, for being the type of person that makes things happen and for consistently adding value to customers/employers. Be the person that sets the standard of performance that customers/employers seek. Be known for your flexibility, innovation in a competitive work environment and a person that your customers/employers can rely on to get the job done.

2. **Grow your contacts** – every quality contact that you add to your network is another building block for your

10 reasons why networking is beneficial:

1. Become better known
2. Grow your contacts
3. Unearth the real facts
4. Building Confidence
5. Guidance
6. Get the edge
7. Career positioning
8. Opinion
9. Ideas
10. Information

continual employability. Each gives you a helping hand towards securing the type of work that you desire. Turn your contacts into long-term relationships. Show a willingness to help them with your expertise and they will return the favour in kind. Every quality contact has something to offer you that you can't offer yourself.

3. **Unearth the real facts** – if you are seeking a move within your company, a promotion or a new job, it is important to find out what the potential position is really like. Use your network to ask the questions that you can't ask at an interview, such as "is the managment good at developing their staff's career, are they support-ive?" In the right circumstances, you can ask any type of question as your contact will usually answer openly. This freedom allows you to discover the reasons for and against a particular job or promotion. Keep probing until you are satisfied that you fully understand the culture, environment and responsibilities of the job.

    If you are considering a switch in your career you could also ask questions about various different indus-tries to build up your market knowledge. This will help to find out what skills are required, how healthy the industry is and what direction it is going in. All this information feeds into your market research.

4. **Building Confidence** – in uncertain times your contacts can give you positive feedback about your employability. They can reassure you and rebuild your confidence, especially if you are made redundant. Your network can also help you deal with any negative criti-cism and make you stronger. Use some of your con-tacts as career supporters and surround yourself with "can do" type people. Your support group will moti-vate and drive you on to achieve your career goals. An effective network will be a rock to lean on when taking on a competitive jobs market.

5. **Guidance** – your network will become a great source of practical advice on how to remain employable. Include

some mentors in your group, as their experience and expertise will be essential. Seek out their opinions on skills and experience that are in demand.

6. **Get the edge** – in today's employment battlefield you need to get the edge on your competition, including your colleagues. Know how to win a job and how to use your network to help. Talent and skill alone won't secure your employment; you must develop a winning mentality and maintain your cutting edge. The extra information that you gather will give you a competitive advantage. Always keep up-to-date with your customers'/employer's future needs. Being employable is about knowing what they want from you tomorrow not what you gave them yesterday. Top sports people always focus on their next game to maintain their winning edge, not on their past glories.

7. **Career positioning** – will ensure that you are moving in the right direction. Use your network to build your awareness of future opportunities and where to position your career. Evaluate what you are currently doing and highlight the areas in which you add value. Look at ways to help key influencers and shine the light on yourself in a positive way. Seek the help of your network in putting yourself in a position that allows you to demonstrate what you can do.

8. **Opinion** – your network group will become a critical and impartial friend. Seek to receive honest and invaluable feedback. You will discover very quickly any errors that you are making with your plans for your future employability. Your network will also offer their opinions on employment trends, how best to market yourself and what customers/employers are really looking for. Quality contacts will always have opinions.

9. **Ideas** – a diverse network group will generate ideas for you. Some of the options offered to you might appear crazy, but the more ideas you have the better

"It is better to have enough ideas for some of them to be wrong, than to be always right by having no ideas at all."

Edward De Bono

the chances are that one will strike the right note. You can adapt these ideas and use them in your business plan. You will learn from other people's experience, both good and bad.

10. **Information** – a good network is a valuable source of information about new opportunities and developments in your field of work. Use the information available through your network to enhance your overall knowledge and understanding of the current jobs market. Your network has free and accessible information that would take years to accumulate on your own.

Networking with professionalism starts before you meet anyone

Increasing your employability options will depend on your ability to network successfully. Productive networking requires careful planning and attention to detail. It is about turning a collection of contacts into employment opportunities in a professional way. People are generally willing to help, provided you don't abuse their time or assistance.

Every time you add a new contact to your network, make sure to note how you were introduced to each other or who your link to each other was.

Every time you add a new contact to your network, make sure to note how you were introduced to each other or who your link to each other was. Otherwise, your new contact might not remember you later.

Before you get in touch with anyone you must carry out some preliminary work in order to get the most from the meeting. You may only get one opportunity to meet with your contact so make sure it's not wasted.

List In the same way that you might compile a list of sales leads, list the people who can help with your employability. Include internal customers such as general staff, colleagues and managers. Then list your external customers, including key people who can influence your career: former work colleagues, teachers/tutors, friends, family, etc.

Purpose Define the exact purpose of each meeting, and your desired outcome. This might sound obvious. However, too many of us get excited when we manage to get an appointment with a key influencer and we forget to focus on what we want from the meeting.

What is it that you want help with? Be as specific as you can. Is it information that you need, or an introduction to someone, or do you simply want to let them know who you are and what you have to offer? Always write down your key objectives and bring them to your meeting. This is your agenda and it will also help you to keep the meeting focused. Each meeting should have a primary purpose, the reason why you set up the meeting in the first place. Always leave the meeting with your primary objective achieved.

Prepare Review all the things you have to do to achieve your goal. Never underestimate the benefits of good preparation and planning. Write down the key questions that you want answers to and the kind of help you need. Keep it concise, as your contact's time is precious.

Do you know what each contact can do for you and what you can offer them? Summarise each contact's profile by answering both of these questions. Practise how you will approach your contact and the way you will talk to them. If you are willing to invest a little time now in innovatively exploring the options that each network meeting presents, you will get back much more in terms of time saved, opportunities created and your employability options improved.

Call As soon as you have finished your preparations make the initial phone call to the contact. Focus on the purpose of the call, otherwise it could become a friendly chat, and of no real benefit to you. If it is a new contact, don't assume that they will instantly know who you are you. Start the conversation by explaining who you are and who introduced you to each other. This should put your contact at ease and make them more willing to meet you. Arrange a meeting for a suitable time and then politely conclude the conversation – don't waste your contact's time with further, unnecessary conversation.

"An amazing thing, the human brain. Capable of understanding incredibly complex and intricate concepts. Yet at times unable to recognise the obvious and simple."
Jay Abraham

Do you know what each contact can do for you and what you can offer them? Summarise each contact's profile by answering both of these questions.

Action Follow up promptly any action that you have decided or agreed to take, organising the venue where you will meet or simply sending on your personal details. Show enthusiasm and gratitude. Take steps to further develop the relationship. Learning from others is a great way to reduce mistakes in career planning.

Networking Profile Sheet

A networking profile sheet is an important item in your networking toolkit. It can form the basis of a simple networking database. It also stores key information about each contact and what you have learned from them. This will help to eliminate any duplication of questions that you need to ask.

Networking Profile Sheet	
Discussion Details	**Details for Contact**
Date: Phone or face to face? Venue: Length of discussion:	Name: Organisation: Job title: Address: Telephone: Email:
Key points for discussion	**Further action recommended**
a. b. c. d.	a. b. c. d.
Action taken? (tick and date)	

The Key to getting the most from your NETWORK	
N	Number
E	Experiences
T	Thankful
W	Who
O	Open mind
R	Rejection
K	Knowledge

N The **number** of quality people in your network group will play a pivotal role in how much benefit you get from career networking. The bigger the pool of people, the greater your chances of stepping closer to a key influencer. Grow your group continually by availing of every opportunity to meet new people. You'll be amazed how many people you meet naturally at social or community events, yet whom you know very little about. Instead of just chatting, learn something new about them. You never know – you could be standing beside the person who will be your next customer/employer.

You never know – you could be standing beside the person who will be your next customer/employer.

E Experiences, both good and bad, are essential to developing and improving your networking skills. After each meeting, whether it went well or was a disaster, you should complete a review document, which will become an integral part of your learning toolkit. Experiences are only worthwhile if you learn from them. Review the purpose of the meeting and whether you achieved your objectives. Think about the type of questions you asked and if you listened carefully to the messages that were given. Always ask yourself what you would do differently next time.

T Thank-you notes should be sent to your contact after your meeting. This gesture will have a positive and lasting impact. Remember your network is helping you and you must express your gratitude both for their time and valuable free information.

W Who are your major contacts and how will they benefit you? Who do I know that could be a link to a key influencer, and how will I get in touch with them? These are just some of the questions you need to ask yourself when growing your network file. List as many people as possible that you know and then "join the dots". You know more people than you think and some can help you more than you realise.

O Maintaining an **open mind** to growing your network list is critical, otherwise you will run out of contacts fairly quickly. Think beyond your family, work colleagues and friends. Be creative and broaden your focus. Always carry your business card as you never know when you might meet a key contact.

R Rejection needs to be managed. Some of your contacts may not be as helpful as you thought, especially some you have banked on. This should not discourage you. Remain focused on the benefits of why you are growing your network and be persistent. Rejection can be good because at least you have discovered that there is no point wasting any further time on that particular contact.

K Knowledge will help you develop a useful and productive network. Establish important facts from every contact in your network file. Find out what careers or industries they are in. Ask each contact who you should talk to in their field and where you can find useful information about their industry. This knowledge is very useful and must be stored carefully. Also be mindful that it is important to pass on your knowledge to others. Think about what knowledge you have that can be useful to them.

Who do I know that could be a link to a key influencer, and how will I get in touch with them?

it is important to pass on your knowledge to others. Think about what knowledge you have that can be useful to them.

Career networking can unearth hidden treasures

Great jobs won't come to you, you've got to get out there and find them. The key to employability is to be proactive and unearth the hidden treasure. These are often missed by people because they rely on the traditional job-finding methods of looking at job adverts and talking to recruitment agencies. While these methods have their place, it is a very crowded market. Treasure seekers look to the hidden market; they look for new adventures.

Discovering these career gems takes a little effort and an entrepreneurial frame of mind. If you are persistent and use your network wisely it can be surprisingly productive. You designed your personal commercial earlier and here is another opportunity to air it to potential customers/employers. Sometimes employers don't realise that they need someone, and that that someone is you. Look for the signs of potential work vacancies such as people retiring or an upturn in staff turnover. Find the job before it goes public and attracts your competitors.

Great jobs won't come to you, you've got to get out there and find them. The key to employability is to be proactive and unearth the hidden treasure.

How to grow your career network to find hidden career gems

It is worth investing a little of your time and energy every week building a network geared towards seeking out hidden career gems. This strategy is important even if you are happy in your current position as you might happen on an opportunity that is too good to ignore.

There are many different approaches you can take to building a good network:

- If relocating is not an option for you to progress your career or find a new job then some old fashioned leg work is a great approach. Get in your car, on your bike or take a stroll around all the business parks and office complexes in your catchment area. Check out the

It is worth investing a little of your time and energy every week building a network geared towards seeking out hidden career gems. This strategy is important even if you are happy in your current position as you might happen on an opportunity that is too good to ignore.

companies in your field and establish which ones are healthy, looking to recruit or who may present hidden opportunities. Talk to the porter, security person or receptionist as they will provide you with key information. Pinpoint key personnel within the company and look at ways of adding them to your contact list.

- Educate yourself in what is happening in your business sector. Establish which companies are expanding, securing large contracts or recruiting. Evaluate the impact that this may have for your current customer/ employer. Read the newspapers, and the Web, and keep yourself informed. Visit these companies and apply for jobs before they are advertised. Make an impact early and always leave with another contact added to your network.

- Tap into new networks by volunteering for work in your local community, or even helping out your local representative. All of these present an opportunity to meet new people. You may also find out what companies are thinking about opening a new office or facility. If you have a lot of free time because you have been made redundant, volunteer to work unpaid for a small business that has a lot of contacts. Trade your skills for their contacts network and perhaps a great reference. Use it to showcase your skills to a new audience.

- Attend conferences and seminars that are related to the type of work that appeals to you. Talk to as many people as possible and find out their needs. Ask for their business cards and follow up later with a call to meet for a coffee and a chat. Develop each relationship slowly to build trust.

You are always networking

Career networking is an ongoing process. You are being judged continually whenever you meet people. It is important to make the most of these meetings. Always have a well-prepared question to ask that will arouse another's interest in you, and remember to carry your business card. If you are between jobs, design your own personal business card. Have a message to communicate and use your network to build your self-promotion skills.

Business networking sites, such as LinkedIn, as well as social networking sites, such as MySpace and Facebook, will also provide you with endless networking opportunities. They are a great way to keep in touch with your contacts. Also, people update their profiles so you can check out when they move from one job to another. Remember to keep your profile up-to-date as you never know who is reading it.

Sending the right signals

Every day you communicate with a wide range of people who can influence your career. These include your work colleagues, superiors and customers. Every time you engage in conversation you communicate both verbally and non-verbally. Non-verbal communication includes the tone of voice and body language such as facial expressions, gestures and eye contact. Interestingly, most people are unaware of using body language when they are communicating. This can lead to mixed messages being sent – we say one thing and our body language says something else. The most common mixed message that can be given when we meet someone for the first time is: "Hi, pleased to meet you", delivered with a weak handshake, bowed head, no eye contact and a facial expression that would turn milk sour. The body language conveys a completely different message, and this will be remembered for a lot longer. When you say you are pleased to meet someone you need to say it and *show* it with conviction.

As we all know, first impressions count and it is hard to overcome a bad first impression. Today we are conditioned to make a strong positive first impression when meeting important people, going for job interviews or going on dates. We put on our best clothes and wear our brightest and most engaging smile. Creating a good first impression is like creating an illusion. However, over time, the real you

According to prominent American psychologist Dr Albert Mehrabian, "we're much more likely to believe that the real meaning is contained in the non-verbal signals the person is giving off, rather than in the words they're saying".

will appear. This can lead to conflict within the relationship if the real you falls short of the standards set by your first impression.

Live up to your positive first impression

Because you are networking all the time, you are also creating first impressions all the time. Start as you mean to go on. Examine the signals that you are giving and make sure that they do you justice. Use the first impressions you make as building blocks. Networking creates an awareness and interest in you; take that initial interest and turn it into a long-term trusting relationship.

Act and appear professional from the first moment that you meet someone. Set high standards and maintain them over the long-term. Show interest and be genuinely helpful to each contact. People will only stay in your network group if they can trust you and feel that the relationship is mutually beneficial.

Start as you mean to go on. Examine the signals that you are giving and make sure that they do you justice.

Raising your profile

You can raise your profile to attract the attention of key decision-makers in a number of ways. It is important that you are creative when it comes to this area of your career. Have a purpose in raising your profile, as this can often help you with your action plan. Employability is about self-promotion and keeping you in your customer's/employer's mind.

For a quick and easy start, save yourself some time and forget about reinventing the wheel. If you want to successfully raise your profile, examine what the high flyers in your organisation or business sector have done. Ask yourself some simple questions:

forget about reinventing the wheel. If you want to successfully raise your profile, examine what the high flyers in your organisation or business sector have done.

- Why do I need to raise my profile?
- How did the successful people around me raise their profile?
- Can I do something similar?

- Who should I network with?
- Who will assist me in raising my profile?
- What are the benefits of raising my profile?

This simple exercise will ensure that you get off to a flying start. Once you have started to market yourself, you will see yourself in a different light. Your self-confidence will grow and you will be able to deal with rejection in a positive way. Other things that you can do to raise your profile include:

- Find yourself a mentor, who will drive you forward
- Join a professional group in your area of expertise
- Become a well-respected specialist
- Volunteer your services as much as possible

You can also raise your profile by writing articles for business and industry-specific journals, newspapers or for Websites and blogs. Talk about things that will interest potential customers/employers. Finish each article with your contact details.

Volunteer your services

Raising your profile should serve a purpose and you should refrain from using it as a vehicle for aimless self-publicity. Instead, raising your profile is about deciding who should know you and how they will benefit from knowing you. So when you volunteer your services make sure that there is a return on your investment.

Volunteering for the sake of it can annoy people and also waste your valuable time. In fact, some potential customers/employers might wonder if you have enough time for work if you are involved in too many groups and associations.

Effective volunteering of your services can open many doors. If you are selective with your choice, you will benefit enormously. You should put yourself forward for committees and projects that have prestige and will bring you to the attention of potential customers/employers or key influencers. Your voluntary work can also add excitement to your

Effective volunteering of your services can open many doors.

day if you are between jobs or stuck in a boring job. You can also acquire or practise new skills while working on stimulating projects.

Find yourself a mentor

Mentoring involves building a long-term relationship with a more experienced person who isn't your line manager. A mentor will encourage, coach, push and counsel you when things go wrong. They will become your role model. A good mentor will guide you through the more complex work issues and also ensure that you look at the big picture and take a longer-term view of your employability. They don't have a vested interest in your day-to-day work, but are more interested in your broader development.

Most people leave it up to their employer to choose a mentor for them through an in-house mentoring programme. This is a risky strategy as it is left to chance that someone who is really great may choose them to be their protégé. Why leave it to luck? Take responsibility for implementing a mentor programme for yourself and carefully choose your own mentor. Moreover, the work environment is so competitive today that you should seriously consider having more than one mentor. Choose them for their expertise and strengths in different areas. Make sure that they add real value to you and that they don't push you in a direction that you don't want to take.

Take responsibility for implementing a mentor programme for yourself and carefully choose your own mentor.

Choosing the right mentor is similar to choosing the right candidate for a job vacancy. Think of your mentor as someone joining your company, "Employability Ltd". Complete a detailed job description, outlining what you want from this relationship. It is essential that you pick the right candidate as your mentor. Take your time and plan thoroughly.

Relationship stocktaking analysis

Building your career network is an ongoing process. Therefore, every three months, or quarter, it is prudent to carry out a relationship stocktaking analysis. This will ensure that your database is up-to-date and meaningful. It also helps to establish who in your network provides you with the greatest help. These are key people and you should ensure that you have built a strong relationship with them.

To carry out a relationship stocking analysis, start by making a list of all the key people you regularly interact with and describe your relationship with each. This list should include your manager and other senior people, peers and other work colleagues, customers and suppliers. Also include your circle of contacts outside of your work environment, such as family and friends and people from your networking group.

Now, compare this list with the list from the previous period analysed to see if there are any new names. New names should get extra attention in order to cement your relationship. Look at ways to stay in touch. You should also make a note if you fail to make contact with someone on the list. Establish the reason why and see if you can get in touch with them immediately. Pay particular attention to key influencers and examine your relationship with them. Did you have a stronger relationship with them this quarter than last quarter? How have they helped you? Have you developed the relationship further? The answers to these questions will feed into your high performance strategic plan and help you get the best out of your network.

> **Tips for Choosing a Career Mentor**
>
> - Write a job description for the role of your mentor
> - Be very clear about what you want from the relationship – use SMARTER goals
> - Ensure there is no previous baggage in terms of their working relationship with your customer/employer
> - Check that the mentor has the necessary experience to help you
> - Is the mentor approachable and willing?
> - Can the mentor open doors for you?
> - What measurement should be in place to ensure the relationship works?
> - Decide what new skills your mentor could help you with

Pay particular attention to key influencers and examine your relationship with them. Did you have a stronger relationship with them this quarter than last quarter?

Join a professional group

Professional groups such as business groups, trade associations, chambers of commerce, alumni or professional bodies, are a great source of support, information and networking opportunities. Join the key groups in your business and local area and be on the inside track. The people you meet in professional groups can help your employability by keeping you

Top Volunteering Ideas
• Social committee work
• Special work projects
• Write articles
• Local school committee
• Help your local elected official
• Unpaid work at a prestige company

informed about job opportunities, impending changes that might affect your work, and industry news. Grab an opportunity to speak at a professional group meeting to show how competent you are in your business field. This is another opportunity to build your profile.

Do's and Don'ts of career networking

DO:

- ✓ **Be a Master**
- ✓ Build a strong network
- ✓ Establish strong mutually beneficial relationships
- ✓ Unearth hidden opportunities through your network
- ✓ Avail of all the benefits of career networking
- ✓ Carry out a relationship stocktaking analysis
- ✓ Join various key professional groups
- ✓ Get a mentor
- ✓ Raise a positive profile

DON'T:

- ☒ **Don't Be a Slave**
- ☒ Don't believe that networking is all about swapping business cards
- ☒ Don't fail to spot networking opportunities
- ☒ Don't send out mixed messages when communicating
- ☒ Don't forget to thank network contacts for their invaluable help
- ☒ Don't jump into a call to a new contact without a focused objective
- ☒ Don't keep a narrow focus on building your network
- ☒ Don't see networking as a one way relationship

Apply one new idea every week to become more employable and successful.

PERSONAL THOUGHTS

What will I do differently tomorrow?

CHAPTER 7
AUDIT: YESTERDAY A SLAVE TO YOUR JOB, TODAY A MASTER OF YOUR CAREER

Quick guide to this chapter

- Sixty minutes that will enhance your life
- Blame culture versus responsibility culture
- Expectancy Model
- "I'm employable" storyboard
- Your personal brand
- Does your personal brand work for you?
- Use your business card
- It's time to break free from your employee way of thinking
- Making your job work for you
- Protect your Employment ASSETS
- What are customers/employers looking for?
- The 24-Hour Rule is a must

Sixty minutes that will enhance your career

Approaching your career with the mindset of an employee is fraught with danger. Rising unemployment, a competitive jobs market and a changing culture in the workplace are signs that a major shift in thinking is needed to ensure

Approaching your career with the mindset of an employee is fraught with danger.

your employability. Finding employment or building your career by relying on what has worked for you in the past is a dangerous strategy. For many people the "nine to five", permanent and pensionable job is now a thing of the past.

To remain employable, you must stop thinking like an employee, because this has no place in today's job market. Innovation and a positive attitude combined with top quality skills are the essential assets that customers/employers need and demand from their existing people and from potential new recruits. *No one is entitled to a job* – you must continually earn the right to work. You must prove that you are an asset for the future and not a potential liability. Developing an entrepreneurial mindset is the bedrock of your employment strategy.

Invest 60 minutes per week in completing the exercises and ideas contained in this book and you will become a true master of your career. It will change your employability status because it will reinforce the key underlying principle in finding and holding onto work, which is to manage yourself and your career using the same skills, techniques and tools that you use when you manage a business.

Innovation and a positive attitude combined with top quality skills are the essential assets that customers/employers need and demand from their existing people and from potential new recruits. No one is entitled to a job – you must continually earn the right to work.

the key underlying principle in finding and holding onto work… is to manage yourself and your career using the same skills, techniques and tools that you use when you manage a business

Stop and ask yourself …

At this stage of your journey you should be very clear about the importance of taking control of your career and your quest to remain employable. Part of the process is to talk to key influencers about your career options. The more options available to you, the easier your decision-making process will be. Golfer Colin Montgomerie made the decision to increase his options in team selection when he took on the role of Captain of the 2010 European Ryder Cup team. He did it by increasing the "captain's picks" from 2 to 3 players, which he could personally choose. This gave him greater control in team selection. He argued that this change would improve his chances of winning back the Ryder Cup because he believed that "options in life are good".

If you are still unsure about discussing your options, here are some simple questions to get you thinking:

The Challenge
Take a strategic view of your career rather than a reactive crisis management view. This requires an entrepreneurial mindset combined with an understanding of simple business concepts and a dedication to take immediate actions that concentrate on key results. It is all about performance. Your reward is a career that you can control and be proud of, while on the flip-side the consequence of not taking action is a career of missed opportunities and regrets.
It's your move

- When was the last time you talked to someone about your career?
- What event initiated the conversation?
- How much time did you spend discussing it?
- Who did you talk to: a friend, mentor, work colleague or your line manager?
- What action did you take as a result of this conversation?
- What were the consequences of this action?
- What would you do differently the next time?
- Have you scheduled a follow-up meeting to discuss your career again?
- What would prevent you from having this conversation again?
- Who will you discuss it with this time?
- Why did you choose this person?
- What will you discuss?
- What would you like to achieve?
- Was it a difficult exercise?

You need to know what you want from your career and turn your many options into real benefits.

At this stage, it is important to revisit your personal vision statement (see Chapter 2). Review your statement and then update it with the career options that are now available to you. Does your statement appeal to your current customer/employer as well as potential new customers/employers?

"The indispensable first step to getting the things you want out of life is this: decide what you want."
Ben Stein, American writer and commentator

Blame Culture Versus Responsibility Culture

Managing your career and future work prospects are your responsibility, not your employer's. Blaming others for your career disappointments will not help you find another job or move up the corporate ladder. An employee mindset is rampant in a blame culture. People who think like employees more often than not fail to take responsibility for their behaviour and failures. They believe that their redundancy or being passed over for promotion is the fault of their boss and their colleagues. They feel that they are controlled by

Managing your career and future work prospects are your responsibility, not your employer's.

People who think like employees more often than not fail to take responsibility for their behaviour and failures. They believe that their redundancy or being passed over for promotion is the fault of their boss and their colleagues.

their circumstances rather than being in control of them. If something goes wrong they waste more time trying to establish who is to blame rather than ensuring that it won't happen again. Blame culture wastes time, energy and resources; it breeds negativity and no employer will want to hire a person with a negative attitude.

Shifting from being part of a blame culture and building a proactive attitude requires people to take responsibility. Blame culture is focused on the past, while responsibility culture is future-based. You cannot change the past, but you can influence the future. It's your career; you are responsible for its success. Developing an entrepreneurial way of thinking helps you to take control of your future employability by cultivating your ability to seek out career-enhancing opportunities. It helps you create the environment that is right for you to perform at the optimum level. Entrepreneurs make things happen, they don't sit around hoping for things to happen.

Developing an entrepreneurial way of thinking helps you to take control of your future employability by cultivating your ability to seek out career-enhancing opportunities.

Use the Expectancy Model

Use the Expectancy Model
Step 1 – Set SMARTER Goals
Step 2 – Find out what you are expected to do
Step 3 – Exceed expectations
Step 4 – High Performance

To take full responsibility for the success of your career you need to understand your customers'/employer's needs at a higher level. This can be achieved by using the Expectancy Model™. This model sets out clearly not only what is expected of you in terms of your targets and work objectives, but also what you need to do to achieve and exceed your objectives.

Step 1 – Set SMARTER Goals Establish your customer/employer overall requirements. Also find out the reason why these requirements are important to them and when they should be completed. Then list a number of key goals that will help you to successfully meet their needs. Arrange them in order of priority.

Step 2 – Find out what you are expected to do SMARTER goals tell you what you have to do. However, the key to high performance is to understand how to achieve these goals. You need to establish from your customer/employer exactly what they expect you to do to complete these goals. Probe them to find out their level of expectation of you.

Step 3 – Exceed expectations This is where you need to be fully effective. Find out what your customer/employer considers as exceeding expectations. This key piece of information will set you apart. It will allow you to work smarter rather than harder as it helps you channel your energy and effort in the right direction.

Step 4 – High Performance The Expectancy Model provides you with a framework to achieve high performance. It outlines what you need to establish from your customer/ employer: their goals, their level of expectation of you and what they judge as exceeding expectations. High performance is about consistently exceeding your customer's/employer's expectations. Surprise them with your excellence.

Expectancy Model™

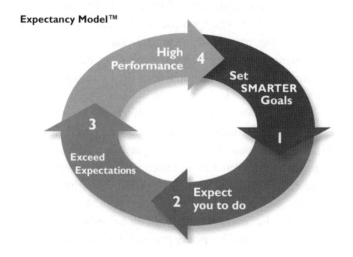

Choose the right path

Remaining employable in the future will be challenging and at times frustrating. It will require persistence, innovation and vision. You will need to accept new ways of working and a different approach to finding work. New work practices, a change in mindset and new skills are now demanded by your

---

The Challenge

- When did you last carry out market research to find out your customer's/ employer's changing needs?
- What exactly does your customer/employer mean when they talk about flexibility, commitment and the need to change?
- Do you know which of your skills are fast approaching their out of style status?
- What do you currently do that justifies your earnings?
- Could you be easily replaced?

This information will give you the edge in your quest to remain employable.

It's your move

customer/employer. Real flexibility and the right attitude are essential qualities. Surviving in the jobs market is about being brave and knowing which path to choose. Millions of people are now at a crossroads in their careers and need to make a decision. When Alice faced the crossroad dilemma, Lewis Carroll brilliantly described the situation faced by so many people:

"Alice came to the fork in the road.

'Which road do I take?' she asked.

'Where do you want to go?' responded the Cheshire Cat.

'I don't know,' Alice answered.

'Then,' said the cat, 'it doesn't matter.'"

> "Alice came to the fork in the road.
> 'Which road do I take?' she asked.
> 'Where do you want to go?' responded the Cheshire Cat.
> 'I don't know,' Alice answered.
> 'Then,' said the cat, 'it doesn't matter.'"

Not knowing where you want your career to go is not an option. There is too much at stake – your happiness, financial stability and employability. You must have a vision of what you want to do with your career and the dedication and commitment needed to turn this vision into your way of life. Long-term employability won't come easy, but it can be achieved by those who know what they want and are prepared to work hard for it.

Self-discipline gives you the ability to persevere with the right course of action even if no one is checking up on you or you would rather be doing something different.

Self-discipline is the process of creating new habits, thoughts and actions towards improving your employability. It gives you the ability to persevere with the right course of action even if no one is checking up on you or you would rather be doing something different. It gives you the strength of character to achieve your goals. Self-discipline will ensure that every day you will do something that adds value to your career. Every day you will think, act and behave like an entrepreneur. Every day you will do something that will ensure your employability.

"Hard work isn't simply the number of hours invested or the number of blisters or bruises incurred. Hard work is also discipline … discipline helps you make the hard decisions. It helps you embrace and endure the pain associated with change. It helps you stay on track despite stress, pressure, and fear."
Vince Lombardi Jr

Take a moment and think about how you can inspire yourself to greatness through self-discipline. What will drive you to success? Is it fear of not having any source of income or the lure of satisfying work? Understand your motivational triggers and start the process of building your career. Remove any blockages to your success and keep a positive mindset.

During your next 60-minute career session start to construct your action plan. The time for talking is over and it is now time to start the doing and building phase. Herb Kelleher, founder of Southwest Airlines, is a firm believer in the principle of doing: "We have a 'strategic' plan. It's called doing things."

"We have a 'strategic' plan. It's called doing things."

Herb Kelleher

Master your Employability

Outline your first steps to greatness

Make your "I'm employable" storyboard

It's time for another of your inspiring storyboards. Creating a storyboard is an excellent way to visually capture your brand and why your customer/employer should buy your services. In simple terms, you tell your story using key words that best describe what you have on offer together with some images that illustrate your story. It is your personal advertisement that spells out clearly the reasons why you are employable. Your storyboard should be a mix of your personal vision statement, some inspiring quotes that will maintain your enthusiasm and motivation, your SMARTER goals for your career and your top three deliverables that will excite prospective customers/employers.

Your storyboard should be bright, full of positive phrases and inspiring. Use the technology that's available to you to help with your design. Finally, create an attention-grabbing headline that will state your strongest benefits and compel people to find out more about you.

Think about your personal brand

As outlined in **Chapter 4**, a positive and strong personal brand will make you more employable and will attract more customers/employers who are willing to pay a premium for your services. You were shown how to build your own personal brand and design a commercial to promote it. It is also important to update your brand appeal regularly before it becomes stale. Here are a few key points to keep in mind in order to maximise the effect of your personal brand:

B	Broaden your focus
R	Review your image and what it says about you
A	Advertise to your target market
N	Network and tell everyone about your successes
D	Develop your communication skills

Broaden your focus

Use every mechanism at your disposal to broaden the reach of your brand. It's not who you know or who knows you that counts, it's who knows you and what you can do for them that makes the difference. You may have a wonderful brand, but if the right people are not aware of you and your brand then you are underselling yourself. Keep yourself in the headlines. Every month you should open up new markets for yourself.

Look at ways of building brand awareness through your networking initiatives, social networking sites, business contacts, family and friends and don't forget the traditional marketing tools. Tell your story in an interesting way to as many people as possible. Refrain from boring people and overselling; excite people instead.

Review your target market and establish whether you have connected with everyone. Add at least one new contact to your list every day.

Ask yourself:

- What's your message?
- Who knows about your message?
- How have you broadened your reach this month?

"Let your hook always be cast; in the pool where you least expect it, there will be a fish."

Ovid

it's who knows you and what you can do for them that makes the difference

Every month you should open up new markets for yourself.

Ask yourself:

- What's your message?
- Who knows about your message?
- How have you broadened your reach this month?

Review your image and what it says about you

Take some time to sit down and think about your brand. Businesses review their brand to ensure that they still appeal to their market. They understand that their brand must communicate effectively their brand essence and what is unique about them.

Ask yourself:

- Are you conveying the right messages to the right people?
- Does your brand spell out clearly that you are flexible, knowledgeable and that you possess the right attitude?
- Does your brand say that you will add value to your customer/employer?

Ask yourself:

- Are you conveying the right messages to the right people?
- Does your brand spell out clearly that you are flexible, knowledgeable and that you possess the right attitude?
- Does your brand say that you will add value to your customer/employer?

Brands need to evolve to meet the changing needs of the market. You cannot stand still and rely on past glories. Review your brand regularly and implement any changes that are required to keep you at the cutting edge. Live your brand and keep up with current trends.

Ask yourself:

- When was the last time you looked in the mirror and reviewed your personal brand?
- Do you check what messages you are sending out at least once a month?
- Are your messages clear and up to date?

Ask yourself:

- When was the last time you looked in the mirror and reviewed your personal brand?
- Do you check what messages you are sending out at least once a month?
- Are your messages clear and up to date?

Advertise to your target market

Use every form of free advertising that's available to you. Write articles, use business networking sites, etc. The growth of new communication media means that you can advertise your brand in many different ways. Check them out and establish which communication channel best suits your needs. Ignite the interest in you by demonstrating your appeal. Excite your customer/employer with a great story that shows them how you add real value to their business.

Sell yourself as an entrepreneur with lots of energy, ideas and a great work ethic. Nobody wants grumpy has-beens in their company; they want bright, positive and knowledgeable "can-do" people. That's what makes people attractive in the work environment today.

Ask yourself:

- What message do you need to send to key people? (Nike has two powerful slogans " Just do it" and "I can")
- How do you advertise yourself?
- Do you grab attention and maintain interest and desire?

Ask yourself:

- What message do you need to send to key people? (Nike has two powerful slogans " Just do it" and "I can")
- How do you advertise yourself?
- Do you grab attention and maintain interest and desire?

Network and tell everyone about your successes

Use social networking sites, business groups and alumni to build a network that will ensure your brand is the one that remains employable. You are only four to five contacts away from somebody who will influence your career in a positive way. The bigger your network, the bigger your customer/employer pool will be. Build mutually beneficial relationships with these people.

Keep everyone you know up to date with your achievements and how these successes can benefit them. They are not interested in your personal glories, but in how you can improve their business. Tell your story from their point of interest.

Ask yourself:

- How many people do I know?
- Who can influence your career?
- How do you get to meet these people?

Develop your communication skills

In order to sell your brand effectively it is helpful if you excel at communication. Being able to speak confidently to your peers and those who are in a more senior position is very important in building a strong brand. Good communicators display assurance and confidence in their abilities and build credibility quickly.

In a competitive market you must be able to grab the attention of a key influencer within the first two minutes. You are not the only person seeking work, so the chances are they have heard all the sales pitches before. Make your pitch memorable for all the right reasons.

Ask yourself:

- How well do you communicate?
- Are you confident using all types of communication?
- Are your career ambitions clearly understood by your target audience?

Ask yourself:

- How well do you communicate?
- Are you confident using all types of communication?
- Are your career ambitions clearly understood by your target audience?

Top 10 questions to determine if your personal brand is working

Your personal brand is constantly evolving; to maintain its competitive advantage ask yourself these important questions. Your answers will guide you through any necessary changes:

1. Where are the similarities between your list of your brand attributes and the lists provided by your mentor or friends?

2. Where are the gaps? What action do you need to take to close these gaps?

3. How does your personal brand meet your customer's/employer's requirements?

4. Do the words that best describe your brand attributes still send out the right messages for today's workplace environment?

5. Do these words label you or place you in a box?

6. Is it beneficial to your quest to remain employable to be placed in this box?

7. What action do you need to take to move to the box that provides the best opportunity of remaining employable?

8. From the list of attributes provided by your mentor or friends, how can you transform any negative words into winning attributes?

9. Have you carried out detailed market research to ensure your personal brand delivers what your current and future customers/employers are looking for?

10. Have you written your winning tag line to reflect your updated personal brand?

Use your business card

If you are out of work, looking to progress your career or looking for a fresh challenge, you will need plenty of personal business cards to give to potential customers/employers. Make it as easy as possible for people to find out about you and what you offer and how to get in touch with you. Design your own business card. On one side display your contact details together with an attention-grabbing headline. For example if you are looking for a new challenge you might use a headline that proclaims your ability such as: "Let me show you how I can outsell 30% of your sales team within one week."

> On one side display your contact details together with an attention-grabbing headline.

On the reverse side, state your top three deliverables that would hook your intended audience. For example, you might say "I have exceeded my sales target by at least 15% in each of the last five years, I have increased market share by 12%" *or* "I build long-term profitable relationships with my clients." Also include any relevant qualifications, industry awards that you have won, and customer testimonials that will enhance your reputation. Keep it concise and memorable.

> On the reverse side, state your top three deliverables that would hook your intended audience.

When a customer/employer shows some interest send them your benefits-focused CV and set up a meeting. Tailor each CV to your potential customer's/employer's requirements and write it from their perspective. Outline your achievements and how these achievements can benefit their business. Take this approach even for your existing customer/employer because it is foolish to expect that they are aware of all of your talents. Invest in some professional help with your CV.

> Outline your achievements and how these achievements can benefit their business. Take this approach even for your existing customer/employer because it is foolish to expect that they are aware of all of your talents.

The positive effect of the SMARTER Way™

During these 60-minute career-enhancing sessions you have set yourself many important goals in order to improve your chances of being employable. It is worth pointing out at this stage that each goal must be set by using the SMARTER Way system. Using the SMARTER Way will have a positive impact on your career and future employability because it will:

- Get you started
- Give you a clear direction on how to remain employable
- Help you get what you really want from your work
- Keep you motivated and focused on being employable
- Clearly state your rewards
- Build persistence which will help you overcome any potential barriers
- Give you the edge
- Ensure that you remain employable
- Energise you

Stay committed to the journey

Maintaining your desire to continually build on your vision requires skill, conviction that you are on the right road and persistence. Breaking free from comfort zones is easier said than done. No long journey is ever without its challenges, and because people put so much energy into the start of their journey they often forget to leave some fuel to finish it.

"All you need is the plan, the road map, and the courage to press on to your destination."

Earl Nightingale

To avoid failing to complete your action plan and to maintain your driving force, you should write a "**4/15 Report**" every Friday afternoon. This report should be brief and uplifting. **Take no more than 15 minutes and answer four key questions**:

- What real value did I add to my customer/employer this week?
- What extra piece of work did I complete this week to keep my competitive edge?
- What did I do to improve my career and employability status this week?
- What are my key SMARTER goals to achieve next week?

Write this report every week and deal with any issues before the end of the following week. This 15-minute habit will keep you on track and in control of your strategy for continuous employability. It is the small actions done on a regular basis that make the big difference over time. In Formula 1 motor racing terms being a second a lap quicker doesn't seem much, but over a 70 lap race it means that you will comfortably win by over a minute. Each small action that you took last week is securing your employment this week, and over the course of a year this mounts up to a considerable difference.

It's time to break free from your employee mindset

The bottom line is that if you continue to maintain an employee mindset you will lose your ability to find work. People who look for the easy option in their workplace are on the road to unemployment. There are very few businesses or organisations left that can afford to carry passengers.

Your ability to break free from your employee mindset is shaped by your personality, attitude and behaviour. Everyone can break free if they really want to. A change in your outlook and way of thinking can be accomplished by:

- Creating your vision for your future career
- Using SMARTER goals to turn this vision into your way of life
- Surrounding yourself with people who have an **entrepreneurial** mindset
- Building your network of suitable contacts
- Exceeding your boss's expectations on a regular basis
- Celebrating your successes
- Creating a positive environment to work in
- Rewarding yourself every time you receive your pay cheque
- Tackling the things that went wrong by turning them into learning experiences

There are very few businesses or organisations left that can afford to carry passengers.

The challenge

What can you do today to create an entrepreneurial mindset?

- List five words that best describe the employee way of thinking. Which ones do you display?
- List five words that best describe an entrepreneurial mindset. Which ones do you display?
- Start eliminating the characteristics of an employee and begin building an entrepreneurial mindset.

It's your move

Making your job work for you

Your current workplace is a source of endless opportunities to drive your career in the direction you want. Maintaining your employment status means you must understand how your job can work for you and add value to your career. Stand back from the narrow focus of your day-to-day work routine and explore the avenues that are open to you. Expand your thinking.

Here are some ways to make your job work for you and therefore improve your employment opportunities:

New internal markets Look for the emerging departments in your company, the ones that do the work that matters. Whose star is on the rise? Which departments are essential to the well-being of the business and which ones can be outsourced, are no longer viable or are over-staffed? Get out of the last three departments fast and move to an income-generating one instead.

Become proactive and use your time wisely. Be decisive. Offer your services for key projects and make a positive impact. Push yourself forward more aggressively. Working on key projects is a great way of displaying your talents in new markets within your organisation.

Join important committees and excel here also. People with an employee mindset often ask the question: "where do you get the time for projects and committees?" In my book *Slave to the Clock, Master of Time*, I show how on average 2.1 hours are wasted each day. Complete a time audit for your working day and find out how much time you really waste per day. This is a revealing exercise as it exposes your true time-wasting activities. Wouldn't it be wiser to spend some of this time working on a project that enhances your employment status?

Customer's/employer's needs As with any business there is one guarantee – your customer's/employer's needs are constantly changing. You must ensure that you are in a position to maximise the opportunities that these changes bring. Carry out your own research to evaluate:

Stand back from the narrow focus of your day-to-day work routine and explore the avenues that are open to you. Expand your thinking.

Which departments are essential to the well-being of the business and which ones can be outsourced, are no longer viable or are over-staffed?

In my book *Slave to the Clock, Master of Time*, I show how on average 2.1 hours are wasted each day. Complete a time audit for your working day and find out how much time you really waste per day.

- Growth areas for your skills, knowledge and expertise
- New markets that your customer/employer might be exploring
- Competitors' changing requirements that might influence your customer/employer
- New products/services that might require what you have to offer

Knowledge puts you in a powerful position and keeps you ahead of your rivals. You must up-skill today for tomorrow's opportunities.

Learn from others

Don't waste time by trying to reinvent the wheel. Instead, observe and learn. Identify people who will become a source of knowledge for you and include your boss in this learning group. Examine how some of your role models became successful, profitable. Learn from their mistakes and successes. Show your current boss your willingness to grow and develop. Let them know your development needs and how they can help you.

If possible, start working with a mentor. A good mentor will guide you into thinking for yourself and finding solutions to business-related issues. It is an opportunity to build powerful and mutually beneficial business relationships. Mentors know how to remain employable and are willing to pass on their tips and experience. They will encourage your goals and provide you with constructive feedback. They have a big picture view of the world and are not hindered by routine work concerns.

> **The challenge**
>
> Once you have conducted the research you need to use that information wisely:
>
> - Align your personal development plan to future trends
> - Update your CV to reflect your findings and outline how you can meet these future needs
> - Demonstrate your flexibility by offering your services to pilot work projects and focus groups
>
> **It's your move**

Circle of influence

Surround yourself with positive and successful people. Build yourself a network of people who will assist your career development. Keep your contacts up-to-date.

If you leave, or other key people leave your organisation,

stay in touch. Build your business alumni. You never know when your paths may cross again, so don't burn too many bridges.

Include junior members of staff in your contact list. New young people are often omitted because you see them in their junior position and not how they can influence your career down the line. However, this is a narrow view, as they may leave your organisation at a junior level but within a few years progress up the corporate ladder. All contacts are important.

You're a winner

If you don't promote yourself, who will? Make sure you take every opportunity to sell your achievements to key people. Gather evidence of your successes and keep them in your "desirable file". Always speak positively about where you work and who you work with. Gather recommendations from people whom you have worked with, or from customers who have been pleased with your performance. These recommendations can lead to powerful referrals.

What are customers/employers looking for?

"In business you get what you want by giving other people what they want."

Alice MacDougall

One of the ingredients in any successful business is to know what the customer wants and then provide it in abundance. This is a simple philosophy, but how many people actually know or attempt to find out what their customer/employer is looking for in their staff? If you know, then you can offer it to them, if you don't then at best you are simply guessing.

Here are some of the qualities that business managers, interviewed as part of the research for this book, are looking for in today's market place.

The challenge

Send an email to 25 potential customers/employers and ask this simple question: "I was wondering if you could help me – I'm looking for the top three things that you look for in an employee, both existing and potential." Then align your offering to their needs.

It's your move

Winning qualities

Attitude The right attitude is the most important quality. Business managers need proactive people who are positive and optimistic. They want people who will give them energy rather than drain it away. The business environment is tough enough, without having to deal with negative and uncooperative people. Possessing the right attitude is a base-line quality that will form the foundation of your employ-ability. It will allow you to develop the key skills that will secure work for you.

The right attitude is the most important quality.

Business managers demand unqualified dedication to the business, a good work ethic and a focus on achieving results. What you put into the job will determine what you get out of it, and it's not just about entitlements and work practice agreements. Managers want passion and a commit-ment to work and a dedication to achieving excellence. They need people who will go the extra distance to get the job done successfully. This type of attitude will set you apart.

"It's never crowded along the extra mile."

Wayne Dyer

Knowledge and experience This is a given in terms of what business managers require. They need people with a minimum basic knowledge of the job and what is needed to perform their key tasks. Relevant experience is always a plus. There-fore, you need to review your current knowledge and experi-ence and see how it can be applied in different work scenarios. Be imaginative and get full credit for all your experience.

Seek out every experience-building opportunity that presents itself and continually update and expand your knowledge. The world is changing too fast to stand still.

"Even if you are on the right track, you'll get run over if you just sit there."

Will Rogers

Ability to analyse situations Foresight and the ability to analyse situations and develop appropriate responses is high on the wish list of potential customers/employers. In wider terms, this is about you understanding the business environ-ment that you are in and how to treat different stakeholders appropriately. This requires a level of maturity that often comes with experience. Watch excellent leaders and learn how they adapt to different, and sometimes difficult, situa-tions. Analyse their approach and understand what worked and what didn't.

Watch excellent leaders and learn how they adapt to different, and sometimes difficult, situations. Analyse their approach and understand what worked and what didn't.

Innovation Nothing stays the same in the business world; as a result customers/employers seek out people who can bring innovation to the workplace. They are not necessarily looking for people as innovative as Steve Jobs (Apple) or James Dyson. They are just looking for people who consistently look for ways to improve work processes, who want to improve customer service and sell more products.

These qualities are displayed by entrepreneurs, such as seeking out new business opportunities, gaps in the market or work roles that could be developed, adding more value to the business. People who bring ideas and suggestions to the table are far more employable than those who have little to contribute.

People who bring ideas and suggestions to the table are far more employable than those who have little to contribute.

Decision-making Employers want people who can make at least basic decisions and act on them, rather than checking every single detail with their business managers. This skill is transferable and will improve your employability. Decision-making is at the heart of business success. Work on improving your decision-making techniques.

"It's in your moments of decision that your destiny is shaped."
Anthony Robbins

Good decision-making skills greatly improve how you use your time. Making good and timely decisions frees up precious time that you can use to add more value to your customer/employer.

Real flexibility means you can adapt to change and do what is required at any given time. This is very challenging for people who have worked for a number of years in a stable business environment.

Flexibility Real flexibility means you can adapt to change and do what is required at any given time. This is very challenging for people who have worked for a number of years in a stable business environment. Very often flexibility wasn't part of their performance evaluation.

Today's work environment requires much more flexibility from people, and as a result you must demonstrate a real desire to be flexible. That means filling in where you are needed most, embracing a fluid working structure and displaying a willingness to work outside your job description. It also means that you meet with customers when it suits them, introduce business processes that are customer focused rather than inward focused and that, where possible, you meet every customer's needs. Customers/employers demand flexibility; it's a basic requirement today.

Energy and enthusiasm Energy and enthusiasm is infectious in a positive way. It sends out the right messages to your customer/employer. Displaying a "how can I help you?" attitude is paramount in delivering quality service. Showing enthusiasm for your work and a passion to deliver results reassures your customer/employer that they made the correct decision in hiring you and that you are the right person to move the business forward today. Ensure your energy is maintained after the initial induction phase.

It is also important to bring some initiative to your job and a desire to keep improving how you do your work. Energising your work environment will also boost morale among your co-workers.

Connecting with people Your ability to satisfy external customers' needs by connecting with people is another quality that is much sought after. The talent to find out what customers want and then give it to them is not to be underestimated. You must demonstrate your willingness to understand, empathise and connect with people at all levels.

When you connect with people you can capture important market-related information which should be fed back to management. Information about impending changes in your customer organisation, relevant information about suppliers and competitors and any industry-related details are all valuable. If you become the source of useful information you will again set yourself apart and be more employable.

A desire to learn Customers/employers are looking for people who have a hunger to learn and are willing to progress within their role. They will also be at an advantage if they display the ability or desire to develop beyond their initial role, through the acquisition of new skills and gaining further experience.

They want people who have ambition and are challenged by their work. They want people to look at how they can grow within the organisation. Employable people never stop learning.

The talent to find out what customers want and then give it to them is not to be underestimated.

Team player You must be a good fit with existing team members and the prevailing business ethos. The overall integrity and effectiveness of the team is of paramount importance. Most organisations need to know that you can get along with people and be a team player.

Ensure that you make the team stronger with your presence. Be helpful to your colleagues and create an environment that is performance focused. If you become a great team player your colleagues will also be singing your praises.

Employment ASSETS™

Throughout this journey you have remodelled yourself by utilising all of your business skills and acumen to ensure your employability for now and the future. It is your ASSETS™ that will drive you forward. ASSETS stands for:

ASSETS stands for:
Attitude
Skills
Service
Experience
Talent
Saleable

> Attitude
> Skills
> Service
> Experience
> Talent
> Saleable

It is critical that you put into practice each component of the ASSETS™ model. These are:

If you have a tendency to fall into the trap of thinking like an employee, try to escape it now. Build yourself a defence mechanism that will alert you to any negativity.

A – Attitude The best way to ensure your employability is to display the right attitude and cultivate an entrepreneurial mindset. If you have a tendency to fall into the trap of thinking like an employee, try to escape it now. Build yourself a defence mechanism that will alert you to any negativity.

S – Skills Always be on the lookout to develop the skills that your customer/employer needs, not only today but, more importantly, tomorrow. Find out what they need and learn these skills. Conduct a regular skills audit. Skills can take a long time to master, so don't waste any time hoping that you won't have to retrain. Embrace new knowledge and demonstrate to your customer/employer that you are flexible and versatile.

S – Service Live and breathe excellence. Know exactly what your customer/employer wants and expects from you. Then endeavour to exceed their expectations as often as possible. Set the standard for performance and make the competition chase you. Challenge yourself to become the market leader in customer/employer service. Outstanding service is a rare commodity and it is remembered long after your interaction with that person. Define what outstanding service is and deliver it every time.

E – Experience Don't confuse length of employment with experience – they aren't the same thing; nor are they equal. Experience is about growing as a person, trying new things and pushing yourself to solve complex problems. People who are constantly looking at ways to gain new experiences and break free from their comfort zones are putting in place the building blocks for their future employability.

> "Those who build their experience build their future."
> Nan S. Russell

To gain valuable experience you must seek opportunities to grow. This can be difficult at first because you leave yourself open to failing in a public way. However, remaining in your current comfort zone carries far more risks than gaining new experiences.

> "There are no failures – just experiences and your reactions to them."
> Tom Krause

T – Talent Your talent is what you are really good at and it drives your success. It is your capacity to take your innate ability and use it to deliver results that will set you apart from the competition. You can create real value for your customer/employer by aligning your talent to their business needs.

In the 1990s a McKinsey study coined the term "War for Talent". Finding people with the type of talent that an organisation requires, and then ensuring that they apply their talents productively is an extremely difficult process. Although the jobs market is competitive and there is an oversupply at the moment, there is still a shortage of real talent. Nurture your talent.

S – Saleable Apply all good selling practices to selling your career. Get you marketing mix right, price yourself competitively and promote yourself at every opportunity. Know your benefits and communicate them to your market. Having the right mix of skills, knowledge and attitude is no good to you unless you can sell it to someone. Remember you are selling yourself all of the time.

The 24-hour rule is a must

This book is full of ideas and suggestions. It has also challenged you to come up with some great ideas and solutions to help you to be employable. However, the world is full of people who have great ideas but few turn them into reality. The reason is simple: they fail to take action.

The 24-Hour Rule is not an option; it's a must. You must complete at least one action that will progress your career within the next 24 hours. It doesn't matter whether the action is big or small. Then, within the next 24 hours you complete another action and so on. Then this will become a new habit of achieving.

> "A year from now you may wish you had started today."
> Karen Lamb

> You must complete at least one action that will progress your career within the next 24 hours.

Write a business journal

A business journal is a simple way to record your progress. It will help you to manage your annual performance reviews as well as providing you with an invaluable document of different projects you undertook. Over time, it will build into a history of your success. It should include:

- Records of your meetings
- Monthly reviews by management
- A documented account of all your successes
- Both good and bad experiences encountered with customers
- An update on a special project that you were a part of
- How people helped you
  Use it as a review document and progress report.

Personal performance audit

Based on the principles of running any type of successful business there is a need to carry out regular personal performance audits. You need to find out where you are and where you are going. Benchmarking against your competitors is a good way of assessing your performance.

Your personal performance audit is based on a series of questions that will help you to push and stretch yourself in order to improve your employability status. Each question needs to be answered honestly. After carefully reading each question rate yourself as follows:

1 Falls below my standards
2 Meets my standards
3 Exceeds my standards

For each question that you score 1 on you must decide on the action that you will take to move your score to the next level. These mini-projects will form part of your business development plan. Initiate your plan without delay

For each question that you score 2 on decide initially on the action you will take to maintain this level and then what action you can take to move your score to the next level. Again these mini-projects will form part of your business development plan.

For each question that you score 3 on you must decide on the action that you will take to maintain this level. This is your preferred state.

Key questions that will improve your employability and show how you excelled this month

Have you added value to your customer/employer this month?

Rating	Action To Be Taken

Have you advanced your career this month?

Rating	Action To Be Taken

Is your personal brand positioned to avail of future opportunities?

Rating	Action To Be Taken

Do you continually look for critical feedback on your performance and learn from both your successes and failures?

Rating	Action To Be Taken

Do you deal with change in a positive and open-minded way?

Rating	Action To Be Taken

Do you spend enough time reviewing your employability status?

Rating	Action To Be Taken

Do you have a clear vision for your career?

Rating	Action To Be Taken

Do you review your business ASSETS™ on a quarterly basis?

Rating	Action To Be Taken

Do you view yourself as a business?

Rating	Action To Be Taken

Have you invested in your business ASSETS™ this quarter?

Rating	Action To Be Taken

Do you have a clear and well-defined picture of your customer's/employer's current and future needs?

Rating	Action To Be Taken

Do you have an entrepreneurial mindset?

Rating	Action To Be Taken

Have you updated your business plan this month?

Rating	Action To Be Taken

Have you stretched yourself this quarter?

Rating	Action To Be Taken

Do you allow procrastination to affect your efficiency
and effectiveness?

Rating	Action To Be Taken

Have you achieved all of the career goals that you set at the
start of the month?

Rating	Action To Be Taken

Do you overcome any obstacles to improving your
employment status?

Rating	Action To Be Taken

Do you deliver the best quality service possible?

Rating	Action To Be Taken

Do you have a strong conviction that your ASSETS™ will
drive better business results for your customer/employer?

Rating	Action To Be Taken

Do you use your networking skills to add value to your career?

Rating	Action To Be Taken

Do you act with a clear understanding of your customer's/ employer's commercial drivers?

Rating	Action To Be Taken

Do you focus on your customer/employer in all that you do?

Rating	Action To Be Taken

Do you motivate and inspire others to a better performance and to continually improve?

Rating	Action To Be Taken

Do you adapt and show flexibility to meet the changing needs of your customer/employer?

Rating	Action To Be Taken

Do you demonstrate a drive to excel, and keep excelling?

Rating	Action To Be Taken

Do you make effective decisions to drive your career forward?

Rating	Action To Be Taken

Did your last performance review meeting add value to your career path?

Rating	Action To Be Taken

Will your next performance review meeting add value to your career path?

Rating	Action To Be Taken

Do you create and deliver new ideas to realistically drive profit growth and opportunities for your customer/employer?

Rating	Action To Be Taken

Do you actively understand your external business environ-ment in order to shape your employability?

Rating	Action To Be Taken

Do you allow the fear of criticism or failure to affect your performance?

Rating	Action To Be Taken

Have you allowed your energy levels to drop due to lack of motivation?

Rating	Action To Be Taken

The seven deadly career sins

There are important career building blocks that can greatly enhance your employability. Equally, there are seven deadly sins that can hamper your career. You need to acknowledge this fact and develop a method of dealing with each of them. These deadly sins are a virus that can slowly kill your ability to find work.

1. Sloth Never underestimate how lazy you can be with your career. You will spend on average 40 of your most productive years working, yet spend more time planning your summer holidays, buying a new car or choosing a new colour scheme for your house than you will spend planning your career.

There are no justified excuses for being lazy with your career. If you suffer from career laziness you need to focus on **Chapter 2**. You also need to take action now. Write down what you need to do to overcome career laziness.

Key Career Sloth Indicators	Action To Be Taken

2. Pride Never let pride get in the way of learning new skills or developing your career. It is not a sign of weakness to ask for help or guidance. As Socrates points out "Employ your time in improving yourself by other men's writings, so that you shall gain easily what others have laboured hard for." Get yourself a mentor who will help to build your knowledge of what it takes to be employable.

If you are out of a job tell the world that you are available. You are only a couple of people away from your next customer/employer. However, if you don't broadcast the fact that you are looking for a job they may not offer you a position. Statically there are more jobs filled through word of mouth than through job advertisements.

Key Career Pride Indicators	Action To Be Taken

3. Anger Becoming angry over a lack of progress or excitement in your career is a definite sign that you are losing your focus. Carrying anger around is a waste of energy. Refocus your anger into a positive force by analysing the root cause of your frustrations, then consider the options that are available to you. Don't beat yourself up over mistakes, learn from them and then move on.

Key Career Anger Indicators	Action To Be Taken

4 Greed Being greedy with your time and experience can alienate your colleagues. This could rebound on you when you require help from others. Help people develop their careers and you will be surprised what you receive in return.

Share your knowledge and experience especially with your young work colleagues. Some day they may be in a position where they can return the favour.

John Quincy Adams once said, "If your actions inspire others to dream more, learn more, do more and become more, you are a leader."

"If your actions inspire others to dream more, learn more, do more and become more, you are a leader."

John Quincy Adams

Key Career Greed Indicators	Action To Be Taken

5. Gluttony Biting off more than you can chew can turn into a poor career move. Taking on too many tasks can leave both you and your customer/employer feeling frustrated when tasks are left incomplete. It is important to know your limits and work within them.

Being over-optimistic about what you can achieve can be as punishing to your career as an employee mindset. Set challenging targets but ones that can be achieved with determination and the deployment of your ASSETS™.

Key Career Gluttony Indicators	Action To Be Taken

6. Lust Lusting after other people's jobs can create many business enemies no matter how discreet you are. Instead turn lust into a positive quality by pursuing new experiences, learning and by providing outstanding service.

"Anyone who stops learning is old, whether at 20 or 80. Anyone who keeps learning stays young. The greatest thing in life is to keep your mind young." Henry Ford

Key Career Lust Indicators	Action To Be Taken

7. Envy Life is about choices. You can choose to have a successful and rewarding career, or you can waste a lot of time thinking enviously of people in cushy and exciting jobs. If your career is failing to challenge you, there is no one to blame but yourself. If you are not employable do something about it today.

Don't waste time or energy on envy. It can make you do strange things and take regrettable decisions. Instead of being envious of someone else's job or career carry out some personal market research. Find out how they got this fantastic job and develop a strategy to find a similar job.

Key Career Envy Indicators	Action To Be Taken

Strategic planning

In your working day you spend a significant amount of time planning your workload, attending endless meetings and thinking about your time off. It's also important to build in some time for planning your career into your working day, week and month. Planning is essential if you want your career to grow and prosper. Put it in your diary as a top priority meeting, book a room and have this essential meeting with yourself every month.

Some of the topics that you can raise at your meeting include:

- Business plan to remain employable
- Review of your personal performance audit
- Analysis of your skills audit
- Jobs market research
- Networking brief

- You own your career so move it in the direction that you want it to go – discuss your action points for the next month.

A final thought

A business without customers has no business; an employee without an employer has no business. Never lose sight of the fact that your employer is your customer. The great thing about your career and ultimately your employability is that you are the master of how it will turn out. You can decide what you want to be and then endeavour to achieve it. It's important that when you write the final chapter in your career journal there are no regrets. As the great comedienne Lucille Ball said:

"I would rather regret the things I have done than the things I have not."

And remember – if you take your eyes off your goals you will only see the barriers, and if you stop listening to your heart you will only hear negative thoughts. Be strong, be brave, be visionary, be happy, be a master of your career.

Do's and Don'ts of managing your career today

DO:

- ✓ **Be a Master**
- ✓ Motivate yourself with SMARTER Goals
- ✓ Utilise your ASSETS™ fully
- ✓ Improve a little every month
- ✓ Seek out new opportunities to build your experience
- ✓ Keep yourself fresh and desirable
- ✓ Use your 4/15 report to remain focused
- ✓ Make your current job work for you
- ✓ Use the 24-hour rule to kick-start your career
- ✓ Be employable

DON'T:

- ☒ **Don't Be a Slave**
- ☒ Don't become complacent about your career
- ☒ Don't undervalue your ASSETS
- ☒ Don't let the seven deadly sins control your career and employability
- ☒ Don't forget to complete your monthly personal performance audit
- ☒ Don't be undecided about what you want from your career
- ☒ Don't blame others if you are unhappy with your current position
- ☒ Don't become unemployable

Apply one new idea every week to become more employable and successful.

PERSONAL THOUGHTS

What will I do differently tomorrow?

REFERENCES

Adams, Scott, *The Dilbert Principle* (HarperBusiness, 1996)

Arruda, William and Dixson, Kirsten, *Career Distinction: Stand Out By Building Your Brand* (Wiley, 2007)

Fayol, Henri, *General and Industrial Management* (Pitman, 1965)

Hartley, Bob and Starkey, Michael W. (eds.), *The Management of Sales & Customer Relations* (International Thomson Business Press, 1996)

Keough, Donald R., *The Ten Commandments of Business Failure* (Portfolio, 2008)

Lees, John, *How to Get a Job You'll Love, 2007/2008 Edition: A Practical Guide to Unlocking Your Talents and Finding Your Ideal Career* (McGraw-Hill Professional; 2007)

Lees, John, *How to Get The Perfect Promotion — A Practical Guide To Improving Your Career Prospects* (McGraw-Hill Professional, 2003)

Lombardi Jr., Vince, *What it Takes to be #1* (McGraw-Hill, 2001)

Porter, Michael, *Competitive Advantage* (Free Press, 1998)

Prone, Terry, and Lyons, Kieran, *This Business of Writing* (Chartered Accountants Ireland, 2006)

Rotella, Dr Bob, *Golf is Not a Game of Perfect* (Simon & Schuster, 1995)

Russell, Nan S. *What is Experience Anyway?* (JobBankUSA.com, 2004)

Schawbel, Dan, *Me 2.0: Build a Powerful Brand to Achieve Career Success* (Kaplan Publishing, 2009)

Sheridan, Pat, *Human Resource Management – a Guide for Employers* (Chartered Accountants Ireland, 2007)

Thompson, Ed and Kolsky, Esteban, "How to Approach Customer Experience Management", *Gartner Research*, December 2004